JESUS

and

Muhammad

MARK A. GABRIEL, PhD

FRONT LINE

A STRANG COMPANY

Most STRANG COMMUNICATIONS/CHARISMA HOUSE/FRONTLINE/ CHRISTIAN LIFE/SILOAM/REALMS/EXCEL BOOKS products are available at special quantity discounts for bulk purchase for sales promotions, premiums, fund-raising, and educational needs. For details, write Strang Communications Book Group, 600 Rinehart Road, Lake Mary, Florida 32746, or telephone (407) 333-0600.

JESUS AND MUHAMMAD by Mark A. Gabriel, PhD
Published by FrontLine
A Strang Company
600 Rinehart Road
Lake Mary, Florida 32746
www.strangdirect.com

Unless otherwise noted, quotations from the Quran are from *The Noble Quran*, English Translation of the Meanings and Commentary published by King Fahd of Saudi Arabia in Medina, "The City of Light," Saudi Arabia in 1998. The translators were Dr. Muhammad Taqi-ud-Din Al-Hilali and Dr. Muhammad Muhsin Khan.

Quotations from the Quran marked ALI TRANSLATION are from *The Quran Translation*, 7th edition, by Abdullah Yusef Ali (Elmhurst, NY: Tahrike Tarsile Quran, Inc., 2001).

Unless otherwise noted, Scripture quotations are from the Holy Bible, New International Version. Copyright © 1973, 1978, 1984, International Bible Society. Used by permission.

Scripture quotations marked NKJV are from the New King James Version of the Bible. Copyright © 1979, 1980, 1982 by Thomas Nelson, Inc., publishers. Used by permission.

Author's note: Having reseached the information thoroughly, I believe the time line of the life of Jesus is best represented as it appears in the *Life Application Bible*, Arabic version (Netherlands: Tyndale House Publishers, 1999). For that reason, any chronological references to the birth, life, and death of Jesus are quoted from this source.

Cover design by Karen Grindley

Library of Congress Cataloging-in-Publication Data

Gabriel, Mark A.
  Jesus and Muhammad / Mark A. Gabriel.
     p. cm.
Includes bibliographical references.
  ISBN 1-59185-291-9 (pbk.)
  1. Muòhammad, Prophet, d. 632. 2. Jesus Christ. 3.
Islam--Relations--Christianity. 4. Christianity and other
religions--Islam. I. Title.
  BP75.G23 2004
  232--dc22

                                          2003026543

ISBN-13: 978-1-59185-291-9

08 09 10 11 12 — 12 11 10 9 8 7
Printed in the United States of America

Dedicated to
the United States of America
and the American people
who opened their country to me
and received me with love.
May this book lead you
to a clear understanding
of the lives and teachings of
Jesus and Muhammad.

Your servant,
Mark A. Gabriel

Contents

SECTION 4
CONCLUSION

Introduction

Without question, Jesus and Muhammad are the two most influential persons who ever lived. Today we can see their influence in the two largest religions in the world: Christianity with more than two billion followers, and Islam with 1.3 billion.

A great chasm exists between these two groups. Most Christians recognize that they have very little understanding of what Muhammad did and taught. Muslims, on the other hand, believe they understand who Jesus was and what he taught, but their beliefs conflict with the teachings of the New Testament.

So here is the question: How can we see a true picture of these two men at the same time?

First, we have to recognize an important principle: we must separate the leader from the followers.

We cannot look to Christians to learn what Jesus taught, nor can we look to Muslims to determine what Muhammad taught. We must not focus on the actions of those who call themselves Muslims or Christians. It does not matter how many terrorists call themselves Muslims, and it does not matter how many Nazis or Crusaders called themselves Christians.

Instead, we must look directly at the teachings and actions of Jesus and Muhammad as they are recorded in the most reliable sources.

There is a big difference between looking at the sources yourself and relying on other people to tell you what those sources say. I believe that is why Muslims do not understand Jesus and Christians do not understand Muhammad.

My purpose in this book is to be your guide and to take you to the original sources so that you can meet these two men for yourself.

You may ask, What makes you qualified to do this? My answer is that I have already met these two men. Though I have a Christian name now, I was born with a Muslim name. Though I have a PhD in Christian education, I also have a PhD in Islamic history and culture from Al-Azhar University in Cairo. Though this book is written in English, my native tongue is Arabic. I have walked in both worlds.

In the Western world, you have many people who are knowledgeable about the life of Jesus. And in the Islamic world you can find many Muslims who are experts about Muhammad's life. But it is hard to find one to speak to the Western world about Muhammad from the original sources. That is why I think I have something unique to offer.

In reference to source information, I strongly encourage you to read Appendix A of this book, which describes the sources that I have used for information about Muhammad and Jesus. If you are a westerner, it will be almost impossible for you to understand the quotes from Islamic sources unless you read Appendix A.

The rest of the book is logically organized to guide you through the following topics:

- In Section 1 I present to you my background and how I came to see the life of Jesus and the life of Muhammad side by side. When I write or speak, I rarely describe my education in detail, but I do so in this book because you should know that the information about Muhammad comes from a qualified source. If you are not interested in reading my story, feel free to skip to Section 2.

- In Section 2 you will read about what Jesus and Muhammad did with their lives. This is where you will find some amazing parallels, such as the fact both men were prophesied over as children, both had cousins who introduced them to the public, both were rejected by their hometowns, and both were assisted by twelve disciples. This section lets Jesus and Muhammad walk side by side, from their births to their deaths.

- Section 3 focuses on the legacy they left behind by their teachings and examples. Profound differences become evident. First you will learn who each man claimed to be and his message to the world. This is followed by a look at what Muhammad said about Jesus and what Jesus might have said about Muhammad. Then we will examine the activities that dominated their lives—for Jesus, healings and miracles; for Muhammad, holy war. Chapters fourteen, fifteen, and sixteen compare their teachings on love, prayer, and women. This section ends with two chapters that focus on quotations that show (1) a comparison of how Jesus and Muhammad reacted in four amazingly similar situations and (2) their teachings on eight key subjects compared verse by verse.

- In Section 4 I give you a summary of the important facts about Jesus and Muhammad and describe what happened to me personally after I saw Jesus and Muhammad side by side.

If you are reading this book in a free country, you are a privileged person. You have the right to explore ideas as you please. Most of those in the Muslim world will never know the information that is in this book. Their leaders will keep it from them. However, both the Bible and the Quran say the truth will prove itself true (Acts 5:33–40; Surah 2:256). So let us examine the facts about Jesus and Muhammad.

Section 1
My Background

1

Growing Up in Islam

It was a beautiful winter day in Egypt. The air was cool, and the sun was shining brightly. I had just finished breakfast at my home where I lived with my mother, father, brothers, sister, grandfather, and uncle. I was five years old at the time, but I remember the day clearly.

My uncle said to me, "We are going to read the Quran together. Do you have your copy?" Eagerly I went to get a slim book that my uncle had given me earlier. It was not the entire Quran, but it was one of the thirty parts.

My uncle had just graduated from the most prestigious Islamic university in the world, Al-Azhar in Cairo. Only in his thirties, he was now the imam of the largest mosque for our area and a man who was revered by all devout Muslims.

We walked hand-in-hand across the street to our family's orchard, which was planted with grapes, figs, and orange trees. The orchard was next to a canal, and when we sat on the bank we could see fishermen, rowboats, and farmers bringing their water buffalo to drink and bathe.

My uncle started reading. The words were familiar because I had heard them all my life—in the mosque, on the radio, and from the Quran reciter that we paid to come to our home. My uncle read the first verse of the last chapter of the Quran. Then he asked me to repeat it back to him. I did so. Then he corrected my pronunciation of the classical Arabic and told me to repeat it to him again. I did so. We did this many times until I had memorized this verse perfectly. Then we started on verse 2.

We went through three or four verses this way. Then we were

interrupted. People always wanted to ask my uncle questions about faith and Islamic law because he was one of the few scholars who lived in our area. While I waited for him, I played down at the edge of the water. Then he called me: "Go back to your mom and ask her to help you get ready to go to the mosque."

I ran back to my house, and when I got inside the front door I heard my grandfather calling, "Come, come," from his room. My grandfather was in his eighties and had gone blind. I was very fond of him, and I ran into his room and kissed his hand as he lay on his bed. Then I jumped up on the bed and gave him a hug. He said, "Tell me: did you read the Quran?"

I said, "Yes."

He said, "Recite to me," and I did.

He was so happy to hear me. "Boy," he said, "I thank Allah for you. You are going to memorize the whole Quran. You are going to be a candle in our home."

I nodded and then slipped out of the room to prepare to go to the mosque. This was Friday, the holy day in Islam when the sermon is preached at the mosque. My mom helped me put on the white robe and skull cap—our traditional clothing for going to the mosque. After my uncle was ready, we walked the half mile to the mosque together as a family. My uncle gave the sermon, and my father, brothers, and I sat in the front line of men. My mother, sister, and other female relatives sat in the back in the women's section.

This is how I remember the day that I began my memorization of the Quran.

A WAY OF LIFE

From that day forward, my uncle became my mentor. He worked with me almost on a daily basis.

When I turned six, he enrolled me in an Al-Azhar primary school. There were fifty secular primary schools in our province, but there was only one Al-Azhar primary school. This elite school focused on a religious Islamic education. None of my brothers or sister went to this school, but there was no jealousy or anger about this. They just were proud and celebrated what I was accomplishing. People began to call me "Little Sheikh."

I did more than meet the school requirements for memorization. Steadily, my uncle was working with me to finish memorizing the entire Quran (which is about the length of the New Testament) at a very early age.

Most mornings I would go with my father and uncle to the morning prayers at the mosque, which started around 3:30 a.m. and finished around 4:30 a.m. (depending on the time of the year). After the prayers, my father and uncle usually went home to sleep two more hours before getting up for work. I usually stayed in the mosque with my copy of the Quran. Before I started memorizing the new verses, I tested myself on the verses I memorized on the two previous days. After I made sure my memorization was OK, I started the new material.

I read the first verse of the passage. Then I closed my Quran and repeated the verse as I walked from corner to corner to corner of the mosque. When I finished the first verse, I opened my Quran and read the second verse. I continued this way until my memorizing was done.

I was very careful to retain what I had learned, so I spent two or three days a month in review. If you asked me about something I had memorized months earlier, it was there in my mind.

AFTER SEVEN YEARS...

Not only did my uncle help me memorize, but he also made sure I understood the classical Arabic—the language of the Quran. The average Arabic speaker cannot read or understand this type of Arabic very well, and learning this language was a crucial part of a religious education.

For seven years my uncle worked with me, verse by verse and chapter by chapter. The year I turned twelve, I completed memorizing the Quran. According to the Al-Azhar educational system,

I was not required to finish memorizing the Quran until I had completed my four-year bachelor's degree at the university, so I was very young.

Needless to say, my family was delighted. They threw a huge celebration for our entire clan in a large hall that was built for our clan's special events. I will never forget my blind grandfather there, calling out for me, "My son, where is my son?" I ran to him, and he just hugged me, tears running down his face.

Having learned the Quran put me in a position to have an unusual amount of respect as a child. People treated me like a holy person because I carried the holy book in my mind.

From that time on, I would systematically read and review the Quran to make sure I did not forget what I had learned.

SUCCESS IN SCHOLARSHIP

When I entered the Al-Azhar high school, one of our main duties was to memorize the most important passages of hadith.

Most westerners do not know what hadith are, so let me explain. The hadith, pronounced *ha-DEETH*, are the accounts of the teachings and actions of Muhammad. These accounts were recorded by his closest followers, his servants, and even his wives. For example, a hadith may describe how Muhammad prayed, how he settled a dispute between two Muslims, or an event that occurred during a battle. Some hadith are only one sentence long, while others are one to two pages. The usual length is about three paragraphs.

Muhammad's followers were very dedicated to keeping the records of what he did and said. There are more than half a million hadith! (For more information, see Appendix A.)

Of course, none of us were going to memorize all of the hadith. But the school had a certain selection of hadith to memorize each semester. On the first day of hadith class, the teacher would pass out the book with the hadith that we were supposed to memorize for that semester. There were several hundred hadith in each book.

We memorized one to three hadith per day during the school year. My uncle also worked with me to memorize additional hadith, and I memorized some extra on my own as well. My uncle was training me to preach in the mosque, which I began doing occasionally even while I was in high school. Upon completing high school I estimate that I had memorized between five thousand and six thousand hadith.

Needless to say, the religious education in high school was very thorough. When students graduated from Al-Azhar high school at the age of eighteen, they were qualified to lead prayers and teach in mosques without any further education.

I was a devout Muslim at this time. My heart was to follow the example of Muhammad in everything I did.

ENTERING THE UNIVERSITY

After my high school graduation, one of my brothers suggested that I attend pharmaceutical school. But the rest of my family urged me to continue my religious study. So I enrolled at Al-Azhar University in Cairo and chose to study in the College of Arabic Language, just as my uncle, who was my mentor, did before me.

Any person from a Muslim background is familiar with Al-Azhar University because it is the most powerful school in the Islamic world. Its influence is difficult to describe to westerners because there is no university in the Western world with an equivalent status. It is amazingly large—up to ninety thousand students at campuses throughout Egypt. It is surprisingly old—the Great Mosque at Al-Azhar was completed in A.D. 972, and academic lectures began three and one-half years later.[1] It is unanimously respected—described in Islamic media as "Sunni Islam's highest authority."

I always enjoyed studying history, so I chose to major in Islamic history and culture. I wanted to learn more about the patience, courage, and commitment of Muhammad and his companions that I admired so much.

On my first day of classes, I received a surprise introduction to the type of education I was about to receive. The sheikh who taught the first lecture of the day was a short man with dark skin, a small moustache, and very thick glasses. He told us: "What I tell you should be accepted as truth. I will not allow any form of class discussion. What I do not say is not worth knowing. Listen and obey, and do not ask any questions."

I was disturbed by this philosophy, and I stood up to speak. The sheikh noticed me right away because I was sitting in the second row. I said, "O master sheikh, how can there be teaching without questions?"

"Where are you from, boy?" he demanded.

"From Egypt," I replied, forgetting that it was obvious that I was Egyptian.

"I know—but from where in Egypt?"

I told him the name of my region, and he retorted, "So, then, you are an ignorant jackass!" He said that because people from my region were looked down on.

I replied, "Yes, I must be a donkey to leave my home and come here and be insulted!"

The class was silent. I slid out of my row of seats and headed toward the door to leave. The sheikh shouted at me, "Stop, you animal! What is your name?"

"It's no honor for me to tell you," I said coldly.

At this the sheikh became enraged and began ranting about crossing my name off the university list and throwing me out on the streets. I left the room and went directly to the dean of the faculty. I told him what happened. After the sheikh was finished with his class, the dean called him into the office.

The dean skillfully convinced the sheikh to forgive me, and he also persuaded me to be more tolerant of him. "Take him to be a father figure," he said, "who only wishes to correct you, not insult you."

This incident introduced me to the way of silence and submission that was demanded at the university. Our method of study was to read the books written by the greatest scholars of Islam, both modern and ancient. Then we would make a list of the key points in each book and memorize the list. We would take written tests for each class, and some teachers would ask for reports. I also read additional Arabic literature and poetry for my own enjoyment.

Even though I knew better, many times I asked questions my professors didn't like.

TOO MANY QUESTIONS

For example, I asked one professor, "Why did Muhammad tell us first to get along with Christians, and then he said to kill them?"

The professor replied, "What the prophet tells you to do, take it as is. What he prohibits, you prohibit. What he allows, you allow. You are not a true Muslim if you do not submit to the words of Muhammad."

I asked another professor, "Why was the prophet Muhammad permitted to marry thirteen women, and we are commanded not to marry more than four? The Quran says Muhammad was just a human being. So why did he have extra rights?"

My professor replied, "No. If you look carefully, you will see Allah gave you more rights than the prophet himself. Allah requires you not to marry more than four. But you have the ability to divorce. So you can marry four today, and divorce them tomorrow, and marry another four. So you can have an unlimited number of wives."

To me, this wasn't a logical answer, especially because Islamic history indicates that Muhammad also had the right to divorce. Muhammad had so much trouble with his wives that one time he threatened to divorce them all.

I even questioned Sheikh Omar Abdel Rahman, well known for being the mastermind behind the bomb attack against the World Trade Centers in 1993. When I was at Al-Azhar, he was the professor for my class in Quranic interpretation.

He gave us a chance to ask questions, so I stood up in front of five hundred students and asked: "Why is it that you teach us all the time about jihad? What about the other verses in the Quran that talk about peace, love, and forgiveness?"

Immediately his face turned red. I could see his anger, but I could also see that he chose to control it. Instead of yelling at me, he took the chance to reinforce his position. "My brother," he said, "there is a whole surah [chapter] called 'Spoils of War.' There is no surah called 'Peace.' Jihad and killing are the head of Islam. If you take them out, you cut off the head of Islam." The answers I received from him and other professors did not satisfy me.

Some people labeled me a troublemaker, but others were tolerant, believing that I sincerely wanted to learn.

At the same time, I excelled in my studies. After four years I graduated second out of a class of six thousand students. This ranking was based on the scores from the oral and written exams that were given at the end of each year of study. The oral exam focused on memorization of the Quran and hadith, and the written exams covered the subjects that we studied in class. Each year you could earn a maximum of fifteen hundred points.

MASTER'S DEGREE AND LECTURING

Before I could begin my master's degree, I spent a mandatory year in the armed forces. After I was finished, I returned to Al-Azhar. I decided at this point that no professor or sheikh was going to help me answer my questions. I would have to find the answers for myself. Doing the research for my master's thesis was a perfect opportunity for this.

I had no one telling me what I was required to read, so I looked at a wide variety of material about Islamic history. Instead of finding answers, however, I became further disillusioned with Islam. Without exaggerating in any way, I can say that Islamic history is a story of violence and bloodshed from the time of Muhammad to this present day. When I looked at the teachings of the Quran and Muhammad, I could see why Islamic history developed this way. I thought, *What God would condone such destruction of human life?* But I kept this kind of question to myself.

My master's thesis created quite a stir. I restrained myself from questioning Islam, but I touched on the controversial issue of what kind of government an Islamic nation should have. The Egyptian government liked my ideas and arranged for a live broadcast of my thesis defense by the Holy Quran national radio station.

From the outside, I appeared very successful. The university asked me to begin lecturing in my area of expertise—Islamic history and culture. At twenty-eight years old, I was one of the youngest lecturers they had ever had. I also led prayers and preached at a mosque in a suburb of Cairo. However, on the inside, I was still looking for truth.

At this point, I was not really in control of my life any more. I couldn't stop and look for another job. The university, my family, my community would ask, Why are you doing this? It would not be logical to leave behind all this education. I had no way to go but continue walking this road. I began to work on my doctorate degree.

2

Leaving the University

I spent two years doing research for my doctorate degree. During this time I had two main responsibilities. I was lecturing for Al-Azhar, both at Al-Azhar University in Cairo and at other Islamic universities throughout the Middle East. And I was the leader of a small mosque. I lead first, fourth, and fifth prayers every day, and on Fridays I preached the sermon and led prayers all day.

I loved teaching and talking to the students. After a while I started a new way of lecturing: I allowed debate, and I let students ask questions. This was a dangerous thing to do. For example, when I taught about the early leaders of the Islamic empire, we came to the story of Muawiya [*Moo-uh-WEE-yuh*] and his son, the subject of my master's thesis. Muawiya was one of the men who transcribed the Quranic revelations for Muhammad, who could not read or write. He became the fifth ruler of the Islamic world after Muhammad. Before his death, he advised his son to hunt down and murder four specific men who would threaten the son's ability to be the next leader of Islam. His son followed his advice; he also went beyond his father's advice and killed the grandson of Muhammad in order to secure his position. I told the students, "Let's look for God in this situation. We need to look for the mercy and love in this situation."

I wanted to establish a new spirit in this class. I was not allowed to have this when I was a student. I wanted them to think freely and use their brains without being afraid of the repercussions.

Most of the students were willing to think critically. One asked, "Is this hadith real? Maybe Jews made it up." I took him back to the source and answered, "It was real. It was not a fake." So they just thought about the question. But the radical students felt that I was accusing Islam. "Allah, forgive us!" they shouted. "You are our professor. Teach us about Islam. You are confusing us."

These students went to the university leaders and said, "This is a dangerous professor. We don't know if he is still a Muslim or if he is a convert."

Al-Azhar has a great fear of a foreign power invading it from the inside. The head of my department called me to meet with him. I thought the university might crack down on me, but I also thought, *These professors know me. They know my heart and desire to learn. They also know my questions are nothing new.*

In our meeting the head of my department discovered the development of my thoughts. He was scared. "My son," he said, "we can't deal with this issue in this way. There are guidelines, and we must submit. We cannot think more than the prophet himself or more than Allah himself. When you are confused, just say, 'Allah and his prophet know the truth.' Put these things in their hands, and go on." But he realized I needed to be dealt with.

I was called to another meeting with the university committee for policy enforcement. The meeting went well in the beginning. They did not want me to go out from the university and criticize Islam.

At first, they showed restraint. They asked me about my life, home, and family. Then they talked about my classes and students. Finally they challenged me: "Why do you ask questions like that? Don't you know you should treat this subject the way we all learn to do? You know a great deal, but no matter how much we learn, we will be far from truth. Have discipline. Talk about what you understand. Where you struggle, say, 'Allah and his prophet know.'"

They asked, "Did you study *The Sword on the Neck of the Unbeliever* like we asked you to?" This was a book that calls for Muslims to accept the teachings of Muhammad without question.

I answered, "I have read it so many times I have almost memorized it like the Quran."

At this point I had a choice. I could deny any wrongdoing, agree to teach the traditional way, and I would be OK. Instead, I told them what I was really thinking. I answered, "Listen. What I tell you now is not because I want to accuse Islam or the prophet. I believe this strongly in my heart. You know me. You love me. Please don't accuse me. Just find a way to help me and answer my questions.

"We say the Quran is directly from Allah, but I doubt it. I see in it the thoughts of a man, not the words of a true God."

The mood in the meeting changed. One man became enraged. He got up from his seat, stood in front of me, and spit in my face. "You blasphemer!" he snarled. "I swear, your mother is a bastard." I could see by the look on his face that had we not been in a meeting with other people, he would have killed me at that moment. "Get out," he commanded.

I stood up to leave. At that moment my whole body was trembling, and I was sweating. I realized that the words I had just spoken were my death warrant. I wondered, *Will they kill me? How? When? Who? Will my family do it? The people from my mosque? My students?*

This was the most horrible moment of my life.

I left the meeting, and I went home. I did not say anything to my family about what happened, but they could see that I was upset about something. I went to bed early that night.

A TRIP TO PRISON

At three o'clock in the morning that same night, my father heard knocking at the door of our house. When he opened the door, fifteen to twenty men rushed past him carrying Russian Kalashnikov assault weapons. They ran upstairs and all through the house, waking people up and looking for me.

One of them found me asleep in my bed. My whole family was awake, weeping and terrified, as the men dragged me out of the front door. They shoved me in the back of a car and drove away. I was in shock, but I knew this was a result of what happened at the university the day before. I was taken to a place that looked like a prison where I was placed in a concrete cell with another prisoner.

In the morning my parents frantically tried to figure out what had happened to me. Right away they went to the police station and demanded, "Where is our son?" But nobody knew anything about me.

I was in the hands of the Egyptian secret police.

ACCUSED OF BEING A CHRISTIAN

For three days the guards gave me no food or water.

On the fourth day, the interrogation began. For the next four days the goal of the secret police was to make me confess that I had left Islam and to explain how it happened. Their pattern was to leave me alone during the day and take me out of the cell at night for interrogation.

The first night of questioning began in a room with a large desk. My interrogator sat behind the desk with a lit cigarette in his hand, and I sat on the other side. He was sure that I had been converted to Christianity, so the interrogator kept badgering me, "What pastor did you talk to? What church have you been visiting? Why have you betrayed Islam?"

He did more than just talk. I have scars from the burn marks on my hands, arms, and face from his cigarette and a hot iron poker to show for that.

He wanted me to confess that I had been converted, but I said, "I didn't betray Islam. I just said what I believe. I am an academic person. I am a thinker. I have a right to discuss any subject of Islam. This is part of my job and part of any academic life. I could not even dream of converting from Islam—it is my blood, my culture, my language, my family, my life. But if you accuse me of converting from Islam for what I say to you, then take me out of Islam. I don't mind to be out of Islam."

The guards grabbed me and took me back to my cell for the day. My cellmate, thinking I was being punished for being an

Islamacist, gave me some of his food and water.

The next night I was taken to a room with a steel bed in it. Always the guards swore at me and insulted me, trying to get a confession from me. They tied me to the bed and beat my feet with whips until I lost consciousness.

When I woke up, they took me to a small tank filled with ice-cold water. They forced me to get in, and it wasn't very long before I passed out again. When I woke up I was lying on my back in the bed where they beat me, still in my wet clothes.

I spent another day in the cell, and the next evening I was taken outside behind the building. I saw what looked like a small, concrete room with no windows or doors. The only opening was a skylight on the roof. The guards made me climb a ladder to the top and demanded, "Get in."

I slid down into the opening and felt the water rise up over my body, but then to my surprise I felt solid ground under my feet. The water only came up to my shoulders. Then I saw something swimming in the water—rats. "This guy is a Muslim thinker," they said, "so we will have the rats eat his head."

They closed the skylight, and I could see nothing. I stood in the water and waited in the dark. Minutes passed. Then hours. The next morning the guards came back to see if I was alive. I'll never forget the sight of the sun as the skylight opened. Through the entire night, the rats climbed all over my head and shoulders. But not one rat bit me. The guards took me back to my cell in disgust.

The last night the guards took me to the door of a small room and said, "There is someone who loves you very much and who wants to meet with you."

I was hoping it was one of my family members or a friend to visit me or get me out of prison.

They opened the door to the room, and inside I saw a big dog. There was nothing else in the room. They shoved me inside and shut the door.

In my heart I cried to my Creator. "You are my God. You are to look after me. How can you leave me in these evil hands? I don't know what these people are trying to do to me, but I know you will be with me, and one day I will see you and meet you."

I walked to the middle of the empty room and slowly sat down cross-legged on the floor. The dog came and sat down in front of me. Minutes went by as this dog looked me over.

The dog got up and started walking in circles around me, like an animal about to eat something. Then he came to my right side, licked my ear, and sat down. I was so exhausted. After he just sat there for a while, I fell asleep.

When I woke up, the dog was in the corner of the room. He ran to me and sat down again at my right side.

When the guards opened the door they saw me praying, with the dog sitting next to me. They were starting to be very confused about me.

This was the last day of interrogation. I was then transferred to a permanent prison. At this point, in my heart, I had completely rejected Islam.

All during this time my family was trying to find out where I was. They had no success until my mother's brother, who was a high-ranking member of the Egyptian Parliament, returned to the country after traveling overseas. My mother called him, sobbing, "For two weeks we have not known where our son is. He is gone." My uncle had the right connections. Fifteen days after I was kidnapped, he came to the prison personally with the release papers and took me home.

A QUIET CHANGE

Some people may say, "Well, no wonder this man left Islam. He was upset because he was tortured by Muslims." Yes, it is true. When I was tortured in the name of protecting Islam, I did not make a distinction between Muslims and the teachings of Islam. So the torture was the final push that separated me from Islam.

But the fact is that I had been questioning Islam for years before

I went to prison. My questions were not based on the actions of Muslims but on the actions of Muhammad and his followers and on the teachings of the Quran. Being in prison just pushed me a little more quickly to where I was already going.

I went back to my parent's house to figure out what I would do next.

Later, the police gave my father this report:

> We have received a fax from Al-Azhar University accusing your son of leaving Islam, but after an interrogation of fifteen days, we found no evidence to support it.

My father was relieved to hear this. He never dreamed that I would leave Islam, and I did not tell him my true feelings. He attributed the whole incident to a bad attitude toward my scholarship on the part of the people at the university. I encouraged him to believe this.

"We don't need them," he said, and he asked me to start work immediately as a sales director for his factory. He had no understanding of my inner turmoil.

3

The Day I Saw Jesus and Muhammad Side by Side

It was time for morning prayers (around 3:30 a.m.), and I could hear the sounds of the household getting up. I was awake, but I had no intention of leaving my room.

It was a few months after I had been released from prison, and I didn't pray at the mosque anymore. Instead of going to the mosque five times a day, I sat at my bed or at my desk, praying for the true God to reveal himself to me, whichever God it was that kept me alive in prison. Sometimes I did not have any words to pray. I just sat and cried. The memories from the prison kept coming back to me.

My mother knocked gently on the door. "Are you going to the mosque today?" she asked.

"No," I said. "I don't want to see anybody."

For the Islamic culture, if you pray in your room, your faith won't be questioned because you are still praying to Allah, which means you are still a Muslim. My family thought that I just needed time to get better. They thought I just didn't want to be around people.

MY INNER STRUGGLE

I came out of prison angry with Islam but convinced that there was an almighty power that kept me alive. Each day, my hunger to find this God increased. All the time I asked myself, *Who could this God be?* I never thought about the God of the Christians or the God of the Jews. Why? I was still influenced by the Quran and Muhammad's teachings. The Quran says Christians worship three gods—God the Father, Jesus the son, and Mary the mother of Jesus. I was searching for the one true God, not three. And the Quran said that the Jews were evil people who had corrupted their Scriptures. So I was not going to look to their God.

This pushed me to look to the religions of the Far East—Hinduism and Buddhism. I had learned about these religions while working on my bachelor's degree, and now I found more books to study about them. Is he the god of Hinduism? I wondered. Is he the god of Buddhism? After my study, I concluded, *No*.

When I wanted to think, I would sit on the bank of the canal and look at the water. Water, green plants, sky, nature—these gave me hope that there was some answer to my questions.

Every day after I finished work with my father, I came back to my home and ate supper with my mother, father, and two brothers who were not yet married. After Thursday supper, it had been my practice to tell stories from the hadith, which my younger brothers loved. I stopped doing this after I got out of prison. My youngest brother was always asking, "Why won't you tell us stories anymore?"

After finishing supper, I went out to spend time with friends. Sometimes I sat in coffee shops, playing games like Dominos or chess. Sometimes I watched sports on TV. Sometimes we walked on the main street along the bank of the Nile River.

I would come back home quite tired around 11 p.m. or midnight. When I was alone again, I felt like the most hopeless person in the world because I had not yet discovered who God could be. I spent one or two hours every night trying to fall asleep. Then I woke up early as usual. My body was tired. I began to have severe headaches.

I went many times to a medical doctor for brain scans. During the day, the headache did not stop me from working and living my life. If I was busy, I could forget about it. But if I was by myself at night, trying to sleep, then the pain was very strong. The doctor prescribed pain pills that I took every night.

The Day I Saw Jesus and Muhammad Side by Side

A New Prescription

I lived this way for about a year. One day the headache was really intense, so I went to the pharmacist again for more pills. Like most of the pharmacists in Egypt, she was a Christian. I had been coming to her for a long time, so I felt comfortable talking to her. I started complaining, "These pills are not working the way they worked before."

She answered, "You are at a dangerous point. You are starting to get addicted to these tablets. You are not just taking them for pain. You are taking them because you can't stop now."

She asked gently, "What's going on in your life?" She knew my family was well respected and that I had graduated from Al-Azhar. I told her I was searching for God. She was surprised. "What about your god and your religion?" she said. So I told her my story.

She pulled a book from the under the counter and said quietly, "I will give you this book. Before you take your tablets tonight, try reading something from it. See how you feel."

I took the tablets in one hand and the book in the other hand. It was a black leather book with the words "Holy Bible" in Arabic written across the front. "OK," I said. "I'll try it." I walked out of the shop and turned the front of the book toward my body so the name couldn't be seen. Then I walked back to my home and went to my room. This was the first time in my life I had ever carried a Bible. I was thirty-five years old.

Reading the Bible

It was a summer night, around 10 p.m. My headache was intense, but I did not take the tablets. I put them on the desk, and I looked at the Bible. I didn't know where to read, so I just let it fall open. This was the pharmacist's personal copy of the Bible, and I noticed her notes on the pages. The pages fell open to Matthew 5.

I started reading at Jesus' Sermon on the Mount. I saw the picture—Jesus on the mountain teaching the crowds around him. As I kept reading, I forgot that I was in my house. I could not feel anything around me. I lost the feeling of time. The Bible took me from story to story through the Book of Matthew.

My brain started working like a computer. In the book on the desk in front of me I saw the picture of Jesus. In my brain I saw the picture of Muhammad. My brain never stopped bringing up the comparisons. I was so full of the Quran and the life of Muhammad that I made no effort to call these things up to my memory. They were just there.

I read the Bible with no awareness of time until I heard the call for morning prayer from the mosque.

READ WITH ME

Dear reader, we have now reached the moment in my life that I wanted you to see. If you want to know what happened to me after this night, you can read it at the end of the book. But I want to stop here for now and review the situation with you.

Here I was, a scholar who had spent thirty years studying Islam and the life of Muhammad. I didn't just practice Islam; I had it memorized. Now I had a Bible in front of me that was introducing me to Jesus.

In the pages you are about to read, I want you to experience what I saw that night in my bedroom in Egypt and what I have continued to discover over the past eleven years. No theology, no commentary, no fancy words. I didn't have someone next to me saying, "This is what the Bible means." I just read what it said for myself. I didn't need someone to tell me, "This is what Muhammad said or did." I had it memorized from the original sources.

Let me introduce you to Jesus and Muhammad.

SECTION 2
THE LIVES OF JESUS
AND MUHAMMAD

4

Childhood Destinies

Muhammad: Born A.D. 570
Jesus: Born 6 or 5 B.C.

As I read about Jesus' life in the Bible for the first time, I was amazed at how many times an event in Jesus' life had a parallel in the life of Muhammad. In this chapter we will walk through the childhoods of both men and discover several of these surprising similarities. Let's start with the fact they were both firstborn sons.

BIRTHS

Muhammad was born in Mecca, Arabia, on August 2, A.D. 570 (the twelfth day of the month of Rabiya on the lunar calendar). Muhammad's father died before he was born, and Muhammad was the first and only child born to his mother. Islamic history records few other details, but there is a story about the night of his birth. This story was told by one of Muhammad's first followers, who said:

> My mother told me that she witnessed Amenah Bint Wahab, the mother of Allah's messenger, giving birth on the night Muhammad was born, and she [Muhammad's mother] said, "Nothing I looked at that night was not of light. I see the stars closing in on me, to where I said they're falling on me."[1]

In other words, when Muhammad was born, his mother declared that the night was so full of light that it seemed as if the stars had come down to earth.

Now let us turn to the story of Jesus' birth. Almost six hundred years earlier, a young Jewish virgin named Mary said the angel Gabriel visited her with news that she would give birth to a child who would be called the "Son of God" (Luke 1:35). As the angel had said, Mary became pregnant, even though she was a virgin. Her pregnancy was a scandal because she was engaged but not yet married. Her fiancé, Joseph, thought that he would end their relationship quietly, but an angel told him in a dream that Mary had become pregnant by the Holy Spirit. During her pregnancy, Mary visited her cousin Elizabeth and told her what had happened. The Bible records her song of praise:

> My soul glorifies the Lord
>   and my spirit rejoices in God my Savior,
> for he has been mindful
>   of the humble state of his servant.
> From now on all generations will call me blessed
>   for the Mighty One has done great things for me—
>   holy is his name.
>
> —LUKE 1:46–49

Elizabeth was also pregnant with a boy—John the Baptist—who would play a key role in the life of Mary's son. Mary stayed with Elizabeth for about three months and then returned to her hometown and to Joseph.

At the end of her pregnancy, Mary and Joseph were required to travel from their hometown of Nazareth to the city of Bethlehem to be registered for the Roman census. It was in Bethlehem that Mary gave birth to Jesus, her first son. The Bible tells many details about the circumstances of the birth.

PROPHECIES OVER BABY JESUS

The stories of Jesus and Muhammad both include prophecies over them as children. Jesus' prophecies occurred when he was still an infant. The Book of Luke tells us that "when the time of their purification according to the Law of Moses had been completed, Joseph and Mary took him to Jerusalem to be presented to the Lord...and to offer a sacrifice" (Luke 2:22, 24).

A prophet named Simeon saw Jesus in the temple. He took him in his arms and said, "Sovereign Lord, as you have promised, you may now dismiss your servant in peace. For my eyes have seen your salvation, which you have prepared in the sight of all people, a light for revelation to the Gentiles and for glory to your people Israel" (Luke 2:29–32).

A woman named Anna came up to them at the same moment, gave thanks to God, and "spoke about the child to all who were looking forward to the redemption of Jerusalem" (Luke 2:38).

Later we will read about a similar prophecy that was given to Muhammad as a teenager.

THE FAMOUS STORY OF MUHAMMAD'S INNER CLEANSING

While there are no stories about Muhammad as an infant, there is a very famous story from his childhood. If you are a Muslim living in the Middle East, you will hear about this story constantly. I estimate that it is mentioned in about 25 percent of all sermons!

> Gabriel came to the Messenger of Allah while he was playing with his playmates. He took hold of him and lay him prostrate on the ground and tore open his breast and took out the heart from it and then extracted a blood-clot out of it and said: That was the part of Satan in thee. And then he washed it with the water of Zamzam in a golden basin and then it was joined together and restored to it[s] place. The boys came running to his

mother, i.e. his nurse, and said: Verily Muhammad has
been murdered. They all rushed toward him (and found
him all right) His color was changed, Anas said.[2]

This story is told to establish Muhammad's special place in the
Islamic faith.

MUHAMMAD'S CHILDHOOD
AROUND AL-KA'BA

Because her husband had died, Muhammad's mother took her
baby and went to live with her family. They were together for six
years until she got a high fever and died. Then Muhammad went
to live with his grandfather on his father's side. His father's family
was part of the Quraysh tribe, the most powerful tribe in Mecca.
This tribe controlled the main place of worship for all of Arabia,
a temple filled with idols known as Al-Ka'ba. Muhammad's grandfather had the honor of serving as the caretaker for Al-Ka'ba. He
was in charge of repairs and cleaning.

The temple was made of a walled courtyard with a large, block
structure in the center. (The phrase *Al-Ka'ba* literally means "the
cube.") The block monument was shaped like a rectangle and
draped with the richest fabrics of the day. Even before the advent
of Islam the people believed Abraham built it. This monument was
also called the Black Stone, in reference to a small stone, believed
to have fallen from heaven, concealed inside the structure. Once
a year Muhammad's grandfather would have removed the coverings, washed the structure, and placed new coverings back on it.

All tribes believed in a supreme god, but they were not sure who
this supreme god was. They looked for a mediator to help connect
them to this supreme god. So they made different types of idols.
The Quran says regarding those idols:

> But those who take for protectors other than Allah
> (say): "We only serve them in order that they may bring
> us nearer to Allah."
>
> —SURAH 39:3, ALI TRANSLATION

Even though each tribe had their own idol to worship, everyone also walked in circles around the Black Stone as part of their worship rituals. However, they did not believe the Black Stone represented the supreme god.

Each tribe had its own traditions for annual pilgrimages as well. So there were always different tribes visiting Al-Ka'ba. When tribes came they gave voluntary offerings of money, food, or animals, which the caretakers and the tribe of Quraysh kept.

As a boy, Muhammad would have often visited Al-Ka'ba with his grandfather or other family members. Care of the temple had been in the family for generations. While Muhammad was still a young boy, his grandfather died, and care of the temple passed to one of his sons, Abu Talib. Care of Muhammad went to Abu Talib as well, so Muhammad went to live with his uncle and cousins.

As he grew older Muhammad continued to spend time around Al-Ka'ba, and he saw the people bowing down to the idols and the businessmen who made a living by making and selling the statues. These experiences had a great effect on Muhammad when he was a young man.

He swore that when he grew up he would never bow down to one of the idols that existed throughout Mecca and Arabia at that time.[3] So we see the influence of the religion of the day upon Muhammad. Let's see how the religion of Jesus' people affected him.

JESUS VISITS THE TEMPLE AS A CHILD

Joseph and Mary were not able to return to their hometown of Nazareth after they had finished registering for the census. This is because some wise men from the East saw a new star and interpreted it as a sign that the king of the Jews that they were waiting for had been born. They went to King Herod in Jerusalem and asked him where they could find this king. King Herod, who was not Jewish and had been appointed as governor by Rome, did not like the idea of another king being born. He called the Jewish teachers of the law and asked them what the Scripture prophesied. They told him that the king would be born in Bethlehem (Matt. 2:5). King Herod told the wise men to find the child and then tell him where he was. The wise men found Jesus, but they did not tell Herod about it.

When Herod realized he had been outwitted by the wise men, he was furious and ordered that all boys under the age of two in Bethlehem and the vicinity be killed. Jesus would have been killed at that time; however, an angel told Joseph to take his family to Egypt. After Herod died, Joseph, Mary, and Jesus returned to Nazareth.

Every year Joseph and Mary and their children traveled to Jerusalem for the Passover Feast. (The Bible says Jesus had younger brothers.) There they would have visited the magnificent temple, which was built by Herod in an attempt to win favor with the Jewish people. It was an awe-inspiring structure made of white stone blocks surrounded by a massive courtyard with colonnades on all sides.

Every year, Jesus returned back to Nazareth with his group. But when he was twelve years old, he sat down to listen to the teachers. His family and friends left at the appointed time, but he could not pull himself away. He stayed, soaking up the teachers' words and asking questions that astounded them.

After a day of travel, his mother and father realized Jesus was missing. They were frantic, and the next morning they retraced their steps back to Jerusalem. For two more days they searched the city, asking if anyone had seen their son. When they found him in the temple, his mother said, "Why did you do this?" Jesus answered, "Didn't you know that I had to be in my Father's house?" (See Luke 2:48–49.)

So Jesus was drawn to the temple while Muhammad became disillusioned by Al-Ka'ba. Now let's see what a Christian priest prophesied over Muhammad.

A CHRISTIAN PRIEST PROPHESIES OVER MUHAMMAD

Muhammad's uncle, Abu Talib, sometimes traveled with one of Mecca's merchant caravans. When Muhammad was twelve, he accompanied his uncle on a trip to Syria. When the caravan reached Syria, they passed by the "cell" of a monk named Bahira. Bahira was part of the Nestorian sect, which meant that he claimed to be a Christian, but he denied that Jesus was the son of God. Most of the people in Arabia who said they were Christians were either Nestorians or Ebionites, both of whom denied that Jesus was the son of God.

So Islamic history says that the caravan reached this priest, who asked them to stop and eat with him. The priest was very interested in Muhammad and asked him some questions. He said Muhammad's responses matched exactly what his books said about a prophet that would come. Then he looked for a mark between his shoulders. When he found it, he told Muhammad's uncle, "Behold, this child is going to be the final prophet for our world. This is the stamp of prophethood." Then he warned, "Don't let the Jews hear about this or see this birthmark on his shoulder. If they find it, they will try to kill him."[4]

What I have presented to you is a faithful record of what Islamic history says about this event. However, there is a difficulty with it from a historical point of view. There are records of what the Nestorians and Ebionites believed. But we have no evidence that they were looking for another prophet.

CONCLUSION

What can we see from the childhoods of Jesus and Muhammad? They were both influenced by the religion of their day and spent time at the worship centers of their regions. They both had reports of prophecies over them as children. While Jesus embraced the beliefs of his people, Muhammad began to question the idol worship of his day. This sets the stage for the beginning of their public lives.

5

The Beginning of
the Revelations

Muhammad: Age 40
Jesus: Age 32

In this chapter you will see what Jesus and Muhammad were doing when they were young men and what happened when they began teaching about a new way of understanding God.

MUHAMMAD WORKS AND MARRIES

Just as it is today, Arabia was a desert in Muhammad's time. This meant that in order to survive, the people needed to trade with other places to obtain food because they could not grow very much themselves. Muhammad's tribe, the Quraysh, were "a people given to commerce."[1] Business leaders in Mecca would send out camel caravans to Syria or Yemen loaded down with goods to sell. When they arrived at their destinations, the caravan leaders would sell their products, use the money to purchase food and other things they wanted, load up the camels, and return back to Mecca.

One of the largest camel caravans was owned by the wealthiest, most powerful woman of Mecca, a lady named Khadija. Islamic history says that when she saw Muhammad's truthful, honest character, she hired him to lead a caravan to Syria. When he returned, the goods were sold for double the investment (or thereabouts). Khadija was impressed. Though she was over forty years old, four times divorced, and had children, she proposed to Muhammad, her twenty-five-year-old caravan manager. People are often skeptical when they hear the account of Khadija proposing to Muhammad. However, this is exactly how the story is recorded in Islamic history. Muhammad's and Khadija's families also struggled with the situation.

Muhammad's uncle who raised him (Abu Talib) and Khadija's father were opposed to the marriage. This is where we see history first mention a key figure in Muhammad's life—Khadija's first cousin. This cousin was known as Waraqa bin Neufal [*Wuh-RA-ka bin NO-ful*]. He was one of the most important religious leaders in Mecca because he was the pastor of the largest church.

You may be surprised to hear about a church in Arabia during Muhammad's time. All the Islamic historical writings, especially the ones relevant to the religious status of Mecca at that time, speak about the arrival of Christianity from the West (Syria, Egypt, Ethiopia, Yemen). Many Arabian tribes embraced it as their religion. However, this form of Christianity was very different from the type described in the New Testament. The two biggest branches were the Ebionites and the Nestorians. Both of these groups denied that Jesus was the son of God or divine.

A large Ebionite church was founded in Mecca by Othman Bin Al-Huweirith. The next pastor of this church was Khadija's cousin, Waraqa bin Neufel.

When Khadija and Muhammad wanted to get married, Waraqa supported them. He convinced both families to let them marry, and he personally performed the ceremony.[2]

So it is possible Muhammad actually had a type of Christian wedding, and his wife was probably also practicing the faith of the Ebionites as well!

Muhammad continued to manage the caravan for Khadija. Even though she was forty years old, Islamic history says they went on to have six children together—two sons who died in infancy and four daughters.

JESUS LIVES QUIETLY

We do not have many specific details about what Jesus did as a teenager or young man. If he had the typical education for a Jewish boy, he would have started to learn to read and write at age five. At age ten, he would have started to learn the Jewish law, or Torah. His formal education would be completed at age eighteen. Because Joseph was a carpenter, Jesus probably learned that trade from him and began to practice it.[3] (He is referred to as the carpenter's son [Mark 6:3].)

Some time before Jesus began to teach publicly, Joseph must have died because Jesus' mother and brothers are mentioned several times in the Gospels, but Joseph is not. Jesus felt responsibility for the care of his mother (John 19:26–27).

We do not have any record that Jesus ever married.

We can make some inferences about his religious life. For example, when he went to the synagogue at Nazareth, he was given the opportunity to read from the Scriptures. He was a familiar sight around the synagogue, participating in worship with the Jews of his area (Luke 4:16).

After he began to preach publicly, the Gospels say that Jesus would go away by himself to pray, so we can assume he was doing this before his public preaching as well.

This is the general picture about Jesus' religious life. Muhammad was also participating in the religious life of his day at Al-Ka'ba in Mecca, as well as spending private time in meditation. Let's take a closer look at how that developed into the first revelation of Islam.

THE REVELATION COMES TO MUHAMMAD

As a young man in his twenties, Muhammad began to travel regularly to a little cave in one of the mountains surrounding the city of Mecca to spend time praying to the unseen god, seeking to see the face of the God-creator. He would spend one, two, or three days at a time in prayer. His wife, Khadija, would bring him water and food.[4]

Muhammad sought people out to discuss their views of God. He became greatly influenced by the Ebionites through his wife, Khadija, and her cousin Waraqa bin Neufal.[5] Waraqa became Muhammad's mentor, teaching him about Christianity. One hadith says that Waraqa used to write parts of the Gospels in Arabic.[6]

Some historical records say that only the Book of Matthew was translated into Arabic at this time, so it is possible that Muhammad was only taught from Matthew. He was also probably taught about the faith of the Jews. The Old Testament teaching was probably limited to the Torah (the first five books of the Old Testament written by Moses) and the Psalms, which were called the Songs of David.

At the same time, Muhammad probably continued to go to Al-Ka'ba. We can infer this because one historian mentions that Muhammad met with Waraqa one time while circling around the Black Stone at the center of Al-Ka'ba.[7]

So at this period in his life, Muhammad was married, leading caravans, learning from his Ebionite cousin, and practicing his personal meditation in the caves around Mecca. He continued this practice for more than fifteen years.

Then at the age of forty (A.D. 610) he had an experience that terrified him.

Muhammad had been meditating during the holy month of Ramadan in the Cave of Hira when, he reported later, "Truth descended upon him."

The angel Gabriel appeared to him and said, "Read!"

Muhammad replied, "I do not know how to read."

The angel caught him and "pressed" him forcefully so that Muhammad thought he could not stand it any longer. Then the angel demanded again, "Read!"

Muhammad replied, "I do not know how."

Again the angel pressed him, and then released him and told Muhammad what to read: "Read! In the Name of your Lord Who has created (all that exists). He has created man from a clot (a piece of thick coagulated blood). Read! And your Lord is the Most Generous."

These were the first verses of the Quran to be revealed. They are recorded in Surah 96:1–3.

How did Muhammad respond to this experience? He said that his heart began to beat severely or "his heart was trembling." His "neck muscles were twitching with terror." He ran back to his wife crying out, "Cover me! Cover me!" They covered him "until his fear was over."

Then he told his wife, "O Khadija, what is wrong with me? What has happened to me? I am afraid for myself." He told her the whole story. His wife realized that she needed some advice.[8]

A CHRISTIAN PRIEST ENDORSES MUHAMMAD'S REVELATION

Here Khadija's cousin enters into the picture again. Khadija went to him and told him what Muhammad had heard and seen. By this time her cousin was an old man and had lost his sight. Waraqa responded, "Holy, holy, holy—I swear in the name of God in whose hand my life is, I swear, Khadija, that this is the great sign that came to Moses, and Muhammad is the prophet of this Arabic nation. Stand and be strong." Khadija came back to Muhammad and told him what Waraqa said.[9]

The next day Muhammad met with Waraqa in Al-Ka'ba, and Waraqa again swore, "In the name of the God who is in control of my life, you are the prophet of this Arabic nation and you received the great signs from God who came to Moses in time past. People will deny you and persecute you and kick you out of your city and fight you, and if I am alive when that time comes [the persecution], I will defend Allah in the way no one can know except Allah himself." And he bowed his head to Muhammad and kissed Muhammad on his face, and Muhammad went back to his house.[10]

Though Waraqa pledged to support Muhammad, he was not able to keep his promise. Either "a few days later" or "a short time later," Waraqa died.[11]

So here we see the picture of Muhammad having an experience in the cave, not certain of its significance, but his wife and her cousin both support the idea that he has been chosen as a prophet of the true God. Let's see what happened when Jesus first presented himself as a prophet.

JESUS AND JOHN THE BAPTIST

Jesus and John the Baptist were connected even before their births. When Jesus' mother became pregnant, she went to John's mother (her cousin) to talk about what had happened to her (Luke 1:39–45).

When Jesus and John were both in their early thirties, John was the first to come into the public eye. He went out into the Desert of Judea and began preaching that people should repent of their sins. People came from Jerusalem and all the region of Judea to see him. When they confessed their sins, he baptized them in the Jordan River.

The Jewish people thought John might be the Christ for whom they were waiting. But John told them, "I baptize you with water. But one more powerful than I will come, the thongs of whose sandals I am not worthy to untie. He will baptize you with the Holy Spirit and with fire" (Luke 3:16).

Then Jesus left Nazareth and came to John to be baptized. The Gospels record:

> As Jesus was coming up out of the water, he saw heaven being torn open and the Spirit descending on him like a dove. And a voice came from heaven: "You are my Son, whom I love; with you I am well pleased."
> —MARK 1:10–11

From that time on, John acknowledged Jesus as the prophet (Messiah) that the Jewish Scriptures foretold.

> Then John gave this testimony: "I saw the Spirit come
> down from heaven as a dove and remain on him.
> I would not have known him, except that the one who
> sent me to baptize with water told me, 'The man on
> whom you see the Spirit come down and remain is he
> who will baptize with the Holy Spirit.' I have seen and
> I testify that this is the Son of God."
>
> —JOHN 1:32–34

John continued to preach and baptize, but people began to
leave him and go to hear Jesus instead. When one of John's disciples complained about this, John told him:

> "I am not the Christ but am sent ahead of him." The
> bride belongs to the bridegroom. The friend who
> attends the bridegroom waits and listens for him, and
> is full of joy when he hears the bridegroom's voice. That
> joy is mine, and it is now complete. He must become
> greater; I must become less.
>
> —JOHN 3:28–30

John's message of repentance did not stop with the common
people. He openly criticized King Herod for marrying his
brother's wife. As a result, Herod locked John up in prison and
eventually beheaded him (Mark 6:14–29).

So we see several fascinating similarities here. Both Jesus and
Muhammad were endorsed as prophets by their cousins, and both
their cousins died shortly thereafter.

THE PAUSE IN THE REVELATION

At the same time Waraqa died, Muhammad's revelations paused.
He stopped receiving visitations from the angel Gabriel.

Muhammad said later that he became...

> so sad…that he intended several times to throw
> himself from the tops of high mountains and every
> time he went up to the top of a mountain in order to
> throw himself down, Gabriel would appear before

him and say, "O Muhammad! You are indeed Allah's Apostle in truth." Whereupon his heart would become quiet and he would calm down and return home.[12]

Muhammad spent one month in the Cave of Hira, seeking more revelations, and then came back down to the valley. As he was walking, Muhammad reported he heard somebody call him aloud:

> I looked in front of me, behind me, on the right of my side and on my left, but I did not see any body. I was again called and I looked about but saw nothing. I was called again and raised my head, and there on the Throne in the open atmosphere he, i.e. Gabriel was sitting. I began to tremble on account of fear. I came to Khadija and said: Wrap me up. They wrapped me up and threw water on me and Allah, the Exalted and Glorious, sent down this: You who are shrouded! Arise and deliver warning, your Lord magnify, your clothes cleanse.[13]

These verses are recorded in the Quran in Surah 74:1–5. After this, the revelation started coming "strongly, frequently, and regularly."[14]

So this could be considered Muhammad's first test as a prophet. Jesus also experienced a test immediately after John the Baptist introduced him as a prophet and "the Lamb of God." Let's look at that now.

JESUS' TEMPTATION IN THE DESERT

After he was baptized by John, Jesus went out into the desert and fasted for forty days. At the end of this time, the Gospel of Matthew says that Satan tempted him three times. First Satan said:

> "If you are the Son of God, tell these stones to become bread."
>
> Jesus answered, "It is written: 'Man does not live on bread alone, but on every word that comes from the mouth of God.'"

Then the devil took him to the holy city and had him stand on the highest point of the temple. "If you are the Son of God," he said, "throw yourself down. For it is written: 'He will command his angels concerning you, and they will lift you up in their hands, so that you will not strike your foot against a stone.'"

Jesus answered him, "It is also written: 'Do not put the Lord your God to the test.'"

Again, the devil took him to a very high mountain and showed him all the kingdoms of the world and their splendor. "All this I will give you," he said, "if you will bow down and worship me."

Jesus said to him, "Away from me, Satan! For it is written: 'Worship the Lord your God, and serve him only.'"

—Matthew 4:3–10

After John was put in prison, Jesus went into Galilee [the region of his hometown], proclaiming the good news of God. "The time has come," he said. "The kingdom of God is near. Repent and believe the good news!"

—Mark 1:14–15

Here we can see that Jesus was confident about his purpose and identity from the very beginning. He was not troubled by his time of testing. In contrast, Muhammad became suicidal when his revelations stopped coming. Now let us see how people responded to the new messages that Muhammad and Jesus presented.

6

The People's Response to the Messages

**Muhammad: The first thirteen years in Mecca.
Age: 40 to 53
Jesus: The first one to two years of ministry up to the time
he sent disciples to preach without him.
Age: early 30s**

At this point in the story, both Muhammad and Jesus have declared that they have been called to present a message from God to the world. Let us look at their first days of preaching. We'll see surprising similarities in the reactions from their hometowns but distinct differences in how Jesus and Muhammad responded.

MUHAMMAD'S QUIET BEGINNINGS

Muhammad's wife Khadija was his first convert to Islam, followed by his ten-year-old cousin (Ali ibn Abu Talib) who lived with them.[1] His next important convert was a former idol worshiper named Abu Bakr. Abu Bakr was quite a successful evangelist for Islam, and he converted twenty-five people, including a man named Al-Arqam. Al-Arqam's house became an important center where Muhammad taught.[2]

Muhammad told the uncle who raised him, Abu Talib, about

his experience, and his uncle committed to protect him, but he did not accept Muhammad's teaching.

So what was Muhammad teaching at this time? He told his nephew that in order to be a Muslim he must "bear witness that there is no god but Allah alone without associates, and disavow al-Lat and al-Uzza [idols], and renounce rivals."[3] Muhammad also said that Gabriel taught him a special pattern for prayer, which he taught to his followers.[4] Later, Muhammad would add new guidelines that must be followed in order to be a Muslim.

In the beginning, Muhammad and the Muslims kept a low profile. They went to the desert valleys outside of the city to pray so that people could not see them.[5] Muhammad continued quietly this way in Mecca for three years.

JESUS' DRAMATIC START

The story of Jesus in the Gospels gives a much different picture about the beginning of his work.

Within a few days after his baptism, five men were already following Jesus wherever he went (John 1:35–40). They went up to Jerusalem together for the Jewish feast of Passover. When they entered the temple courts, Jesus did something that would put him in the eye of the Jewish religious leaders for the rest of his life. When Jesus saw men selling cattle, sheep, and doves and changing money, he became angry. He made a whip and drove every man and animal out of the temple courtyard, shouting, "Get these out of here! How dare you turn my Father's house into a market!" (John 2:16).

The religious leaders questioned his authority, but they couldn't stop him. He stayed in Jerusalem for the Passover feast and did "miraculous signs," which caused many to believe on him (John 2:23). The Jewish religious leaders (the Pharisees) began to keep track of his activities (John 4:1).

Jesus began to speak in Jewish synagogues, and "news about him spread through the whole countryside....everyone praised him" (Luke 4:14–15). After teaching in several different cities,

Jesus returned to teach in his hometown, Nazareth, which was a small farming village of about two hundred people.

So what was Jesus teaching at this time? When he stood up to teach at the synagogue in Nazareth, he was handed the scroll of Isaiah. He read to the people.

> The Spirit of the Lord is on me, because he has anointed me to preach good news to the poor. He has sent me to proclaim freedom for the prisoners and recovery of sight for the blind, to release the oppressed, to proclaim the year of the Lord's favor.
> —LUKE 4:18–19

As the people stared at him, he began to teach them by saying, "Today this scripture is fulfilled in your hearing" (Luke 4:21).

Just days earlier in Jerusalem Jesus had told a religious leader that God "gave his one and only Son, that whoever believes in him shall not perish but have eternal life" (John 3:16). A woman at a well in Samaria told Jesus she was looking for the coming Messiah of the Jews, and Jesus said, "I who speak to you am he" (John 4: 26). In short, Jesus said he was the son of God and that he held the keys to having a right relationship with God that would result in eternal life. This was Jesus' message from now to the end of his life. (We will compare the messages of Jesus and Muhammad in more detail in chapter 10.)

MUHAMMAD REJECTED BY HIS HOMETOWN AND RELIGIOUS LEADERS

Muhammad spread his message quietly for three years until he reported that Gabriel commanded him to speak out the message publicly (at age forty-three). Muhammad decided to call together the leaders of the tribe of Quraysh and tell them about his teachings. There are a few things to remember about the Quraysh: (1) Muhammad's family was part of this tribe. His branch was called Beni Hashim. (*Beni* is the Arabic word for *tribe*.) (2) This tribe generated income by maintaining Al-Ka'ba, the center of idol worship for Arabia.

When Muhammad told them his message, they were offended. They said to Muhammad's uncle, "O Abu Talib, your nephew has cursed our gods, insulted our religion, mocked our way of life and accused our forefathers of error; either you must stop him or you must let us get at him."[6]

Because Muhammad's uncle was protecting him, the people of Mecca could not kill Muhammad, so they harassed him. For example, they warned people who were visiting Mecca to ignore Muhammad. They insulted Muhammad when he walked in circles around the Black Stone in Al-Ka'ba.[7]

The converts to Islam were in more danger than Muhammad himself. The Quraysh put strong pressure on converts to renounce their faith. If the convert was a person who had high standing in society, they mocked him. If he was a merchant, they threatened to boycott him. And if he was a low-class person, they beat him.[8]

Most of the converts were lower class or slaves. However, over time, two powerful men joined with Muhammad—Umar and Hamza (one of Muhammad's uncles). These men were physically strong and aggressive, which intimidated the Quraysh. To weaken the Muslims, the Quraysh decided to boycott the Muslims and all of Muhammad's clan (Beni Hashim).

They signed an agreement that the rest of the tribe should not marry Beni Hashim's women or give women to them to marry. Also, they should neither buy from them nor sell to them.

The leader of the boycott was a man named Abu Lahab, who was another of Muhammad's uncles. He went to the market and told the people, "O businessmen, raise your price very high so the people of Muhammad cannot buy anything from you. If someone worries about the business he will lose, I have enough money to cover it."

Muhammad reported revelations from the angel Gabriel renouncing this man (Surah 111).

After a while Muhammad and the Muslims left the city to go live in the desert valley next to it. They were becoming desperate. When one Muslim went into the city to buy food for his family, the merchants asked him to pay two, three, or four times more than normal. He could not pay, so he went back with nothing for his family.

Islamic history says that Muhammad's people became so hungry that they ate the dung of animals and the leaves from trees. This became known as the Year of Hunger.

Think of it: Muhammad and his wife Khadija, once the richest, most respected woman in Mecca, were refugees in the desert, not even able to buy food. They probably had some of their little children with them as well. They survived on supplies brought to them secretly by sympathizers and friends.[9]

All during this time, Muhammad spoke of revelations from the angel Gabriel. These verses were collected and would be a part of the book known as the Quran. The revelations often contained rebukes toward those who were persecuting him.

JESUS REJECTED BY HIS HOMETOWN AND RELIGIOUS LEADERS

We've seen how Muhammad's hometown rejected him. Now let us look at Nazareth, the tiny village where Jesus was raised. You read earlier about how Jesus stood up in the synagogue at Nazareth to read the Scriptures. Now let us see how the people reacted.

After Jesus read the passage from Isaiah, he continued to teach. He talked about how the people of his hometown Nazareth wanted him to do miracles for them as he had done in Capernaum. "I tell you the truth," he continued, "no prophet is accepted in his hometown." Then he reminded them about Old Testament prophets who were sent away from Israel to help non-Jews. These words made the people in the synagogue furious. They took Jesus to a cliff outside of town in order to throw him off the edge. But Jesus walked through the crowd and went on his way (Luke 4:14–30).

In addition to his hometown, Jesus was rejected by other cities and groups of people. Jesus performed many miracles in other cities of Galilee, but they rejected Jesus' message (Capernaum, Matt. 11:23; Korazin and Bethsaida, Luke 10:13). Jesus' message was particularly offensive to the religious leaders of the Jews, just as Muhammad's message was particularly offensive to the idol worship leaders in Mecca.

The religious leaders of Jesus' day were also trying to kill Jesus, but they went about it differently than the Quraysh in Mecca. Instead of killing Jesus directly, they looked for a way to make him break a law so that they could put him to death "legally." For example, if he committed blasphemy, Jewish law said he could be put to death. If he committed treason against the Roman government, then he could be executed as well (Matt. 22:15).

In the face of rejection, Jesus' pattern was to state his point of view and move on (Luke 9:51–56). As we progress through the lives of Jesus and Muhammad, we will see that Muhammad's reaction to rejection was quite different. Let's see how Muhammad recovered from his tribe's boycott.

THE BOYCOTT IS REPEALED/ MUHAMMAD SEEKS PROTECTION

After two or three years, without any direct intervention from Muhammad, the leaders of the Quraysh decided to repeal the boycott. The leaders decided it was wrong to treat their own relatives so badly, and they tore up the agreement. Muhammad and his people returned to Mecca and continued to practice Islam there, though still subject to some harassment.[10]

Muhammad presented his message by telling people that they must leave their idols, accept Allah as the one true God, and accept Muhammad as Allah's prophet. He would quote verses from the Quran for people as well. When people asked for a sign, he responded, "The Quran is the sign for you" (Surah 29:50–51).

The events of the next few years show that Muhammad was developing a new strategy for establishing Islam and protecting himself.

The People's Response to the Messages

Within a year or two, two very important people in Muhammad's life died—his uncle Abu Talib, who protected him against his enemies, and his wife Khadija, who provided moral support (A.D. 620). Muhammad was fifty years old. Islamic history says that the Quraysh began to treat him "in a more offensive way than before." An example is cited of "a young lout" who "threw dust on his head."[11] However, no direct physical attacks are mentioned—such as beatings, attempted murder, or anything like that. Nevertheless, we can say for sure that Muhammad felt threatened because he went out to find other people or tribes who would protect him. (His followers were seeking protectors for themselves as well.) Islamic history says he traveled outside of Mecca to the people of Thaqif, the tents of Kinda, and the tents of Kalb and was rejected by them all.[12]

When tribal leaders came to visit Mecca, Muhammad would meet with them. He would tell them that he was a prophet and ask them to "believe in him and protect him until Allah should make clear to them the message with which he had charged his prophet."[13]

Except for a few lower-class believers in Mecca, Muhammad's efforts met little success. He finally found his opportunity through the longstanding war between the two major tribes of the nearby city of Medina—Aous and Khazraj. These tribes came to Al-Ka'ba in Mecca for the yearly pilgrimage to worship their idols. After they were finished with their idol worship, some representatives met with Muhammad at night at al-Aqaba. Muhammad told them, "I invite your allegiance on the basis that you protect me as you would your women and children." One of the leaders responded:

> I swear in the name of him who sent you with the truth, we will defend you as we defend our families. Sign this agreement with us, O apostle of Allah. I swear we are the children of war [i.e., we know how to defend you]. We inherit that from generation to generation to generation.[14]

So we see a people who had been established in warfare for many years pledging their allegiance to Muhammad. Muhammad was clearly making a military agreement with these tribes. He told them, "I will war against them that war against you and be at peace with those at peace with you."[15]

At this point we see an ironic similarity with Jesus. Muhammad told the people with whom he was meeting, "Bring out to me twelve leaders that they may take charge of their people's affairs." They produced nine from one tribe and three from another. So Muhammad chose twelve key people to work with him, just as Jesus called out twelve disciples to walk with him.

At this point, Muhammad had spent thirteen years preaching Islam. Now he began preparations to make a major change.

Let's compare this picture from Muhammad's life with how Jesus presented his message.

Jesus Relies on Preaching and Healing

We have progressed through the first half of Muhammad's life as a prophet, and we are now going to focus on the first half of Jesus' ministry. We'll define this as the one to two years that he spent teaching the people and training his disciples before he sent them out on their own.

So, how did Jesus present his message? He traveled from city to city around Galilee and Judea and preached. How did he persuade people to believe him? He healed sicknesses, caused demons to leave people's bodies, and performed natural miracles.

For example, at the very beginning of his ministry, he cast a demon out of a man who interrupted his sermon at the synagogue in Capernaum (Luke 4:33). Then Jesus went back to Peter's house and healed Peter's mother-in-law, who had a high fever. By nightfall a crowd had gathered at the house. They brought to Jesus all kinds of people who had various sicknesses, and he healed them by "laying his hands on each one" (Luke 4:40).

This kind of activity earned him enthusiastic responses from people wherever he went. People brought to him "those suffering severe pain, the demon-possessed, those having seizures, and the paralyzed, and he healed them" (Matt. 4:24). A man whom he healed of leprosy spread the news so effectively that Jesus could not even go into cities openly because of the crowds of people. He stayed outside in "lonely places," and yet the people came to him there (Mark 1:45).

After a miracle of multiplying food, the people began to say, "Surely this is the Prophet who is to come into the world." They were ready to "make him king by force," so Jesus went to the hills by himself (John 6:14–15).

He also became known for his manner of teaching. Matthew said, "The crowds were amazed at his teaching, because he taught as one who had authority, and not as their teachers of the law" (Matt. 7:28–29; see also Luke 4; Matt. 13:54). Jesus often taught people by telling earthly stories with spiritual meanings (parables; Matt. 13:34). For example, to teach the people about forgiveness, he told the story of a servant whose master forgave him a great debt (Matt. 18:21–35).

Near the end of the first year Jesus selected twelve men out of those who had been following him (Matt. 10:1; Mark 3:13; Luke 6:12). These twelve became his closest companions. Jesus would soon instruct them on how to spread his message themselves.

Muhammad also began to work with his twelve new leaders to prepare them to spread Islam throughout Arabia. Let's see what he did.

7

Spreading the Message

**Muhammad: The first seven years in Medina.
Age: 53 to 60
Jesus: The final one to two years of ministry up to
his final journey to Jerusalem.
Age: 34 to 35**

Jesus practiced his ministry the same way from beginning to end. But in Muhammad's life, there was an event that marked a major change. It was the flight from Mecca to Medina known as the *hijra*. In this chapter we will see what happened after Muhammad's move and how he worked with his twelve leaders to spread Islam. We will also see how Jesus worked with his twelve disciples to spread his message.

We will also look at a major subplot in their lives—the opposition they encountered from the Jewish communities or religious leaders of their day.

Muhammad's Army Spreads Islam

In the last chapter, we left Muhammad just after he completed his treaty with the two strongest tribes of Medina. At this point, he began sending his followers in small groups from Mecca to live in Medina. This took a few months.

Muhammad weeps over Mecca

When Muhammad was ready to personally emigrate from Mecca to Medina, he went to the top of the mountain that overlooked Mecca and said, "O Mecca, I swear you are the closest city to my heart, and if it weren't for your people who forced me out, I wouldn't have left."[1]

In other words, Muhammad was saying how much he loved Mecca. Remember Muhammad's words because we will revisit them when he returns to Mecca eight years later.

After this, Muhammad and one of his most loyal followers, Abu Bakr, left Mecca at night and made it to Medina safely. This is known as the second *hijra*, or pilgrimage.[2] The Islamic calendar marks dates according to A.H., or after *hijra*. Therefore a date such as A.H. 5 refers to the fifth year after Muhammad immigrated to Medina.

After years of seeking protection, Muhammad was now in a position of safety. What did he do?

Permission to fight

In Mecca, Muhammad had spent thirteen years being cooperative and tolerant, not driven toward violence. He frequently forgave those who hurt him and did not try to take revenge. After he moved to Medina, this soft lamb turned into a roaring lion.

Before the end of his first year in Medina, Muhammad announced that Allah had given him permission to fight. Islamic history records:

> Then the apostle prepared for war in pursuance of God's command to fight his enemies and to fight those polytheists who were near at hand whom God commanded him to fight. This was thirteen years after his call.[3]

During the first couple of years in Medina, Muhammad led some raids personally, but he also sent his relatives and loyal followers on raids of their own. This included sending his Uncle Hamza with thirty soldiers to ambush a caravan from Mecca and sending a cousin to attack some members of the Quraysh tribe as they were traveling outside of Mecca.[4]

The people of Mecca did not organize any large-scale attacks on Muhammad after he left Mecca. However, Muhammad ordered an attack against a large caravan from Mecca that had gone out to Syria and was returning home. This was a major turning point in the history of Islam.

This attack was more than just economic; it was an attack against Mecca's survival. The caravans went out only twice a year. They returned with food, sugar, salt, and clothing that the people needed to survive. Mecca was in a desert where the people couldn't produce very much food, so they really depended on trade. If Muhammad had succeeded in his attack on the caravan, Mecca would have suffered from many shortages.

As it was, the leader of the caravan, Abu Sufyan, heard about Muhammad's plot and avoided the place where Muhammad was waiting in ambush. (Remember this man because he will be a part of Muhammad's story again later.) The people of Mecca decided, however, that Muhammad needed to be punished for his intentions. They went to fight him, and the two parties met in the Valley of Badr. Muhammad only had about three hundred men, but they won a surprise victory and killed or captured many of the Meccans (Battle of Badr, A.D. 624, A.H. 2).[5] This made him the strongest leader in Arabia. (Even though he had defeated their army, the city of Mecca remained under the control of the Quraysh at this time.)

The Battle of Badr brought holy war to a whole new level. Muhammad said that the angel Gabriel came to him with new revelations about how to handle their success. This is surah 8 of the Quran, titled "The Spoils of War." This chapter talks about the battle and gives some practical instruction. Let's look at four key points.

1. The revelation told Muslims how to divide the goods that they captured from the defeated army.

> And know that out of all the booty that ye may acquire (in war), a fifth share is assigned to Allah, and to the

Messenger, and to near relatives, orphans, the needy, and the wayfarer.
—SURAH 8:41, ALI TRANSLATION

In other words, Muhammad took 20 percent (part of which he could distribute to those in need), and the remaining 80 percent was divided among the people who fought with him. This sounds pretty good when your army has three hundred people, but later his army had up to ten thousand men. With an army that size, each fighter only got .008 percent compared to Muhammad's 20 percent. This caused some complaints among the soldiers.

2. The revelation commanded Muslims to continue to fight anyone who rejected Islam.

Fight them until there is no more *Fitnah* (disbelief and polytheism, i.e. worshipping others besides Allah) and the religion (worship) will be for Allah Alone [in the whole of the world].
—SURAH 8:39

O Prophet (Muhammad)! Urge the believers to fight. If there are twenty steadfast persons amongst you, they will overcome two hundreds...because they (the disbelievers) are people who do not understand.
—SURAH 8:65

The only way to be safe from Muhammad's army was to accept Islam.

Say to those who have disbelieved, if they cease (from disbelief), their past will be forgiven. But if they return (thereto), then the examples of those (punished) before them have already preceded (as a warning).
—SURAH 8:38

3. The revelation told Muslims to prepare for future missions.

> And make ready against them all you can of power,
> including steeds of war...to threaten the enemy of
> Allah and your enemy.
>
> —SURAH 8:60

4. The revelation commanded them to "fight hard."

> O you who believe! When you meet (an enemy) force,
> take a firm stand against them and remember the
> Name of Allah much (both with tongue and mind), so
> that you may be successful.
>
> —SURAH 8:45

Muhammad taught that his mission was to spread Islam through the use of holy war. He gave his followers authority to attack unbelievers and seize their belongings.

MECCA TRIES TO STOP MUHAMMAD

All of Arabia felt threatened by Muhammad. In A.H. 5, some idol worshipers from Mecca joined with some Jews from Medina to attack Muhammad. The Muslims dug trenches around the city of Medina and successfully discouraged the Meccans, who retreated. Almost no fighting occurred. Known as the Battle of the Trench, this event is very important in Islamic history because if Muhammad had suffered a decisive defeat, the future of Islam would have been threatened.

As it was, Muhammad continued to spread Islam through his military. He personally accompanied the fighters on twenty-seven raids, and in nine of those he was on the battlefield fighting along with them. The Muslims conducted a total of thirty-eight raids and expeditions while Muhammad lived in Medina.[6]

Muhammad continued to report revelations from the angel Gabriel during this time. These messages were collected and added to the Quran, as before. The new revelations called for spreading Islam by force.

Now, let's turn to Jesus near the end of his life and see how he instructed his disciples to spread his message.

JESUS SENDS HIS DISCIPLES TO SPREAD THE GOSPEL

Unlike Muhammad, who changed greatly after he moved to Medina, Jesus did not change his message or method of spreading it. As he entered into his third year of ministry, he continued to travel, speak in synagogues or public places, heal the sick, cast out demons, and perform other miracles. The common people were drawn to him, and most religious leaders felt threatened by him. In this setting, he gave his twelve disciples instructions for going out without him to spread the gospel. Later he called a larger group of seventy two to do the same things. Let's look in detail at what he told them.

Travel instructions

As I present Jesus' instructions to his disciples, I will put them in perspective with the instructions that Muhammad gave his people.

1. Muhammad gave his people authority to wage war, but Jesus gave his disciples a different kind of authority. The Book of Matthew says:

   > He...gave them authority to drive out evil spirits and to heal every disease and sickness.
   > —MATTHEW 10:1

   After giving them authority, Jesus commanded his followers to:

   > Heal the sick, raise the dead, cleanse those who have leprosy, drive out demons.
   > —MATTHEW 10:8

2. Muhammad gave his people instructions about how to divide the goods that they seized from unbelievers. Jesus forbid the disciples to ask people for money or to carry money with them.

> Freely you have received, freely give. Do not take along
> any gold or silver or copper in your belts.
> —MATTHEW 10:8–9

But Jesus allowed his followers to stay in people's houses and
eat with them.

> Stay in that house, eating and drinking whatever they
> give you, for the worker deserves his wages.
> —LUKE 10:7

3. If a city rejected Islam, Muhammad ordered the
    Muslims to attack it. Jesus said:

    > If anyone will not welcome you or listen to your words,
    > shake the dust off your feet when you leave that home
    > or town. I tell you the truth, it will be more bearable
    > for Sodom and Gomorrah on the day of judgment
    > than for that town.
    > —MATTHEW 10:14–15

In other words, Jesus said the cities that rejected his message
would be punished by God on Judgment Day, not by the disciples
in the present life.

Just as he did in his own life, Jesus told his followers to walk
away from those who were against them.

> When you are persecuted in one place, flee to
> another.
> —MATTHEW 10:23

4. Muhammad told his people to fight hard against unbe-
    lievers. Jesus told his followers be ready for unbelievers
    to fight them. He said that they would be flogged,
    arrested, and put on trial (Matt. 10:16–19).

The disciples followed Jesus' instructions.

They went out and preached that people should repent.
They drove out many demons and anointed many sick
people with oil and healed them.

—MARK 6:12–13

CONFLICTS WITH THE JEWISH PEOPLE

There is a major subplot in the stories of both Jesus and
Muhammad—their conflicts with Jews or Jewish religious leaders.
Most of Muhammad's interaction with the Jewish people occurred
while he was in Medina because Mecca had few Jews. Jesus, who
himself was a Jew, interacted with the Jewish people all his life.
But he experienced the most conflict with Jewish religious leaders.
Let's look first at what occurred in Muhammad's life.

Muhammad's conflicts with the Jews

The largest Jewish community in Arabia was in Medina. After
Muhammad moved there, he interacted with Jews every day. He
did business with them, visited their homes, and ate with them.

Muhammad expected the Jews to accept Islam because he
taught there was only one God, just as the Jews believed. However,
the Jews were not impressed by Muhammad's teachings. They
wanted him to show them a sign that he was true prophet. The
Quran records:

> And they say: "Why are not signs sent down to him
> from his Lord?"
>
> —SURAH 29:50

Muhammad's response was that he was only a man, a warner,
and that the Quran itself was the only sign people needed.

> Say: "The signs are only with Allah, and I am only a
> plain warner." Is it not sufficient for them that We
> have sent down to you the Book (the Quran) which is
> recited to them?
>
> —SURAH 29:50–51

Muhammad debated with the Jews for three years. Then to everyone's shock, he ordered the assassination of a well-known Jewish man who had been criticizing him with poetry (A.H. 3). Here's how the event occurred.

In a meeting with some of his followers Muhammad asked, "Who will kill this man for me?" Some Muslims volunteered. One evening, they went to the man's house and invited him to take a walk with them. After they had walked and talked for a while, one Muslim gave the signal, and they attacked the man with swords and a dagger, stabbing him to death.[6]

Muhammad's attitude toward the Jewish people had changed. He ordered another assassination and, because they refused to accept Islam and posed a threat to him, he systematically routed them out of Arabia.

First, he attacked the Beni Nadir (tribe of Nadir, A.H. 4). He destroyed their date palms and forced the people to leave the village. Two years later he called for a raid on the village of Beni Qurayzah [Kor-AY-zuh]. He put them under siege. After they surrendered, he killed all the men (about six hundred) and took the women and children as slaves (A.H. 5).[7] Finally, he drove the Jews out of Khaybar (A.H. 7), a Jewish village near Medina.

Muhammad supported himself and his family with the property he seized from the Jews of Khaybar.

> It has been narrated on the authority of Umar, who said: "The properties abandoned by Banu Nadir were the ones which Allah bestowed upon His Apostle for which no expedition was undertaken either with cavalry or camelry. These properties were particularly meant for the Holy Prophet. He would meet the annual expenditure of his family from the income thereof, and would spend what remained for purchasing horses and weapons as preparation for Jihad."[8]

Muhammad would not tolerate criticism from the Jews, and he would not allow them to live in peace for fear that they would join his enemies to fight against him.

Jesus' encounters with Jewish religious leaders

Six hundred years before the time of Muhammad, the Jews of Jesus' day were also critical of a new message. "The Pharisees and the teachers of the law began to oppose him fiercely and to besiege him with questions" (Luke 11:53).

Just as they did with Muhammad, the Jews asked Jesus for a sign.

> Then some of the Pharisees and teachers of the law said to him, "Teacher, we want to see a miraculous sign from you." He answered, "A wicked and adulterous generation asks for a miraculous sign! But none will be given it except the sign of the prophet Jonah. For as Jonah was three days and three nights in the belly of a huge fish, so the Son of Man will be three days and three nights in the heart of the earth."
>
> —MATTHEW 12:38–40

Jesus used the "sign of Jonah" to say that he would die and remain in the grave for three days before he came back to life.

Jesus also offered his healing power and miracles as a sign that he had divine power. When Jesus was teaching his disciples he said, "Believe me when I say that I am in the Father and the Father is in me; or at least believe on the evidence of the miracles themselves" (John 14:11; see also Matt. 9:2–7).

Jesus showed frustration and anger with the religious leaders. The Gospels record several times when he spoke out against them forcefully (Matt. 23; Mark 7:1–23; John 8:42–59). He also used parables to protest their actions (Matt. 21:28–46; 22:1–14). However, he did not attempt to cause physical harm to any of them.

Now that we have seen what Jesus and Muhammad did in their public lives during the second half of their ministries, let us take a brief look at their personal lives.

PERSONAL LIVES

After Muhammad moved to Medina, his personal life changed significantly. While in Mecca, he had remained married to only one wife, Khadija, who died after twenty-five years of marriage. During his first year in Medina, Muhammad signed a marriage contract with the daughter of one of his most loyal followers, Abu Bakr. This would not seem unusual except that the girl was only six years old.[9]

Islamic history says that Muhammad did not consummate the marriage with the girl, named Aisha [*Ah-EE-sha*], until she was nine, but this arrangement was highly unusual, even in Arabian society. She remained married to Muhammad until his death, when she was eighteen years old. However, she was not his only wife. Muhammad married eleven others during his years in Medina. Muhammad spent a fair amount of energy managing his wives. (I explain the impact of his wives in more detail in chapter 16.)

In contrast, we have no record that Jesus ever married. He spent his time with his disciples and was particularly close with three of them—Peter, James, and John (Matt. 17:1; Mark 5:37; 14:33). He maintained his relationship with his mother and brothers, and he also had a close relationship with Mary, Martha, and their brother, Lazarus. A small group of women traveled with Jesus and assisted him. (See chapter 16 for more information.)

CONCLUSION

We are now approaching the end of the lives of both Jesus and Muhammad. The next chapter of this book will look at the final three years for Muhammad (age 61 to 63) and the final few months for Jesus (around age 35 or 36).

8

Last Days

**Muhammad: The last three years of his life.
Age: 60 to 63
Jesus: The final months of his life.
Age: 35 to 36**

As the end of their lives approached, both Jesus and Muhammad were at the height of their influence. In this chapter you will see:

- Their triumphant entrances into cities that had rejected them
- Final instructions to their followers
- How each one died

MUHAMMAD RETURNS TO MECCA

Eight years after immigrating to Medina, Muhammad had reached a new height of power. He had ten thousand soldiers in his army by this time, commanded by four division leaders and himself.[1] Years earlier, when the people were harassing him in the marketplace of Mecca, Muhammad had warned them, "O people of Mecca, I swear in the name of Allah I come as a slaughterer."[2] He was now ready to take action on those words.

As Muhammad's army advanced, the desert was black with horses and men. The city of Mecca sent out spies, including Abu Sufyan, the leader of the caravan that Muhammad had tried to attack when he first left Mecca. This man was captured and, as he stood before Muhammad, chose to convert in order to save his life. To rescue this leader's dignity, Muhammad said that during the attack, Muslims would protect anyone who took refuge in this man's house. He sent the man back to Mecca with this message: "He who enters Abu Sufyan's house is safe. And he who shuts his door upon himself will be safe and he who enters the mosque will be safe." When the people of Mecca heard this, they dispersed to their houses and to the mosque.[3]

When he was about to enter the city, Muhammad called the Ansar fighters to come to him. The Ansar were those from Medina who had converted to Islam, not those from Mecca. When they had surrounded him, Muhammad said, "Do you see the soldiers of Quraysh (from Mecca)?" He made a gesture with his hand and commanded, "Go and slaughter them." The Arabic word for slaughter presents the picture of a farmer harvesting his crop with a scythe. In other words, Muhammad was telling them, "Cut their necks from their bodies as you would cut the fruit from the branch of a tree."[4]

Muhammad's reason for choosing the Ansar for this task was probably because the Muslims who were from Mecca may have struggled with killing their own tribespeople and former neighbors.

As the soldiers entered the city on horseback, some women ran out and hysterically began hitting the horses in the face with their fists, begging the soldiers not to kill them and their children. They were weeping and trying to push the horses back. Imagine this scene! The people were terrified and desperate.[5] Mecca put up little armed resistance, and Muhammad easily took control.

Muhammad's division carried a special flag. It was black with a single word written in Arabic: *punishment*.[6]

Muhammad takes control of Al-Ka'ba

Muhammad rode his horse through the streets of Mecca as the people of the city stayed in their houses. He entered Al-Ka'ba, kissed the Black Stone, and began to walk in a circle around it.

When he reached one idol that was near the Black Stone, he pierced its eyes with his bow that he held in his hand. After noon prayers that same day, Muhammad ordered that all the idols that were around Al-Ka'ba be collected, burned with fire, and broken up.[7] The Muslims would now maintain Al-Ka'ba (Surah 9:18).

Now let us see what happened when Jesus returned to Jerusalem, the home of the chief priests and teachers of the law who were trying to kill him.

JESUS RETURNS TO JERUSALEM

During the final months of his third year of ministry, Jesus was also at his peak of influence and popularity. At the same time, he warned the disciples that he would be killed when he went to Jerusalem.

> From that time on Jesus began to explain to his disciples that he must go to Jerusalem and suffer many things at the hands of the elders, chief priests and teachers of the law, and that he must be killed and on the third day be raised to life.
> —MATTHEW 16:21; SEE ALSO LUKE 13:31–35

> And the disciples were filled with grief.
> —MATTHEW 17:23

Despite the disciples' protests, Jesus continued to make his way to Jerusalem in order to be there for the Passover feast. When he arrived at the city, he made his entrance in a surprising way.

He asked his disciples to find a young donkey for him, and Jesus rode it into the city. As he went along, crowds lined the road. Some people threw their cloaks on the path in front of him, while others cut branches and threw them on the path. They noisily praised God, and the whole city of Jerusalem was stirred up (Luke 19:28–44; Matt. 21:1–11).

Jesus weeps for Jerusalem

As Jesus approached Jerusalem and saw the city, he wept because he knew Jerusalem's future. He lamented:

> If you, even you, had only known on this day what
> would bring you peace—but now it is hidden from your
> eyes. The days will come upon you when your enemies
> will build an embankment against you and encircle you
> and hem you in on every side. They will dash you to
> the ground, you and the children within your walls.
> They will not leave one stone on another, because you
> did not recognize the time of God's coming to you"
> —LUKE 19:41–44; SEE ALSO MATTHEW 23:37–39;
> LUKE 13:34–35

Jesus' prophetic words were fulfilled in less than forty years. In A.D. 70 the Roman general Titus conquered and destroyed Jerusalem and burned the temple to the ground.

So now we have both Jesus and Muhammad at the end of their lives returning to the cities that housed the center of spiritual life for their peoples. Muhammad returned as a conqueror. As we shall see, Jesus returned as a sacrifice. In the last section of this chapter, let's see how these two leaders died and what they gave as their final instructions to their followers.

ARABIA SUBMITS

After the conquest of Mecca, people from all over Arabia who had not yet been attacked sent messengers to Muhammad saying, "We submit to you." Islamic history records forty-eight different groups who submitted to Muhammad in this year (A.H. 9). There were only a few pockets of resistance in Arabia, which Muhammad successfully subdued.[8] The conquered people paid *zakat*, a tax that was 2½ percent of a person's income.

Muhammad sends letters to foreign rulers

Now that Muhammad had conquered Arabia, he contacted the rulers of countries outside of Arabia and called for them to accept Islam and Islamic rule. He sent official letters with his personal seal to the (1) emperor of Rome, (2) king of Iran, (3) king of Ethiopia, (4) Roman governor of Egypt, (5) king of Oman, (6) king of

Bahrain, (7) king of Syria, (8) king of Yemen.[9] These letters warned the rulers to submit to Islam or suffer the consequences. A good example is the letter to the emperor of Rome, which read:

> From Muhammad, the apostle of Allah,
>
> To Herocles, the great one of Rome,
>
> Convert to Islam and you will be saved. And if you reject my challenge, you are responsible for what will happen to you and your people.[10]

Muhammad used the word *saved* in reference to being saved from his army, not in reference to being spared from God's wrath on Judgment Day.

Remember the twelve leaders Muhammad had chosen earlier? Most of them were now leading raids against those who refused to submit to Islamic authority.

New revelations about Jihad

In this setting, Muhammad reported new revelations regarding treatment of nonbelievers. These are recorded in Surah 9. Let's look at two of these verses:

In reference to the *Mushrikun*, or idol worshipers, the revelation was:

> Kill the *Mushrikun* wherever you find them, and capture them and besiege them, and lie in wait for them in each and every ambush. But if they repent and perform *As-Salat* [prayers] and give *Zakat* [charity tax], then leave their way free.
>
> —SURAH 9:5

So this revelation told Muslims to fight idol worshipers until they accepted Islam. A similar revelation was given regarding Jews and Christians with one important difference.

> Fight against those who (1) believe not in Allah, (2) nor in the Last Day, (3) nor forbid that which has been forbidden by Allah and His Messenger (Muhammad)

(4) and those who acknowledge not the religion of truth (i.e. Islam) among the people of the Scripture (Jews and Christians), until they pay the *Jizyah* [tax] with willing submission, and feel themselves subdued.

—SURAH 9:29

Muslims could give Jews and Christians three options.

1. Accept the message of Islam.

2. Remain Jews or Christians but pay a special tax (jizyah), which was traditionally levied once a year.

3. Prepare to be attacked.

Muhammad set up governors (called *amirs*) to rule over all the people, tribes, and areas that accepted Islamic authority (A.H. 9).

MUHAMMAD'S FINAL SERMON ON MOUNT ARAFAT

Now that he had control of Mecca, Muhammad called on all Muslims to participate in a great *hajj*, which was an annual pilgrimage to Al-Ka'ba to worship Allah (Surah 3:97). He spent a year making preparations for a huge event, sending messengers to all parts of Arabia telling people to come. The culmination of this massive gathering was when Muhammad stood on Mount Arafat and preached his last recorded sermon, surrounded by more than one hundred thousand Muslims.[11] This is very well-known as the Sermon on Mount Arafat.

Here is the text of what Muhammad said as recorded in Islamic history.

> Today your religion is completed, and the grace of God is fulfilled in your life. And I bear witness that Islam is your religion. O Muslim people, you are prohibited to shed blood among yourselves or to steal from each other or take advantage of each other or to steal the women or wives of other Muslims.

After today there will no longer be two religions
existing in Arabia. I descended by Allah with the sword
in my hand, and my wealth will come from the shadow
of my sword. And the one who will disagree with me
will be humiliated and persecuted.[12]

This sermon has two parts: The first part teaches Muslims how to
deal with each other, for example, not to murder or steal each other's
wives. The second part teaches them how to deal with non-Muslims.
Muhammad declared that Allah sent him with a sword and that his
income would come from it. He promised humiliation and persecution for those who disagreed with him. (This sermon stands in great
contrast to Jesus' Sermon on the Mount, where Jesus said: "Love
your enemies and pray for those who persecute you" [Matt. 5:44].)

MUHAMMAD'S DEATH

In the eleventh year after his immigration from Mecca to Medina,
Muhammad became ill with the fever he would contract annually.
This time his illness was very serious.

According to Islamic history, Muhammad blamed his fevers
on a poisoning attempt that occurred just after Muhammad
conquered the Jewish village of Khaybar four years earlier. He
agreed to spare the lives of the people who remained if they would
turn over all of their property to him. In this setting, one of the
Jewish women named Zainab prepared a meal for Muhammad.
(Remember, the Jews had a relationship with Muhammad for
years before he decided to subdue them.)

Zainab prepared a lamb (or goat) on the barbecue. She found
out that Muhammad preferred the shoulder meat, so she put
extra poison there, but she poisoned the whole lamb as well. She
brought out the meat and served it to Muhammad and one of his
friends. Muhammad took some of the shoulder meat and began
to eat it, but he tasted something unusual with the meat. He took
it out of his mouth and threw it away. But his friend liked the meat
and ate it. He later died from the poison.

Muhammad asked Zainab about what she had done. She replied, "You know what you have done to my people. I said to myself, 'If he is a king I shall ease myself of him, and if he is a prophet he will be informed (of what I have done).'" For this answer, Muhammad spared her life.

However, Muhammad believed that the poison he ate bothered him for the rest of his life. In his last time of sickness, before his death, the sister of the man who died from the poisoned lamb came to visit him. Muhammad told her, "O Umm Bishr, what you see in me now [my illness] is the result of my eating from the lamb that I ate with your brother."[13]

During his final illness, Muhammad experienced fever and pain for twenty days and was nursed in the house of his wife Aisha, who was now eighteen years old. When he became too ill to lead prayers, he ordered that his trusted followers perform that task. When he was drawing his final breaths, he laid his head on Aisha's lap and died.[14]

Muhammad was buried in Medina, and pilgrims still visit his grave today.

JESUS' DEATH

The story of Jesus' death is very different than Muhammad's. Let's see what happened.

Jesus had gone to Jerusalem to celebrate the feast of Passover. The chief priests and teachers of the law were looking for some way to get rid of him, but they were afraid of confronting him directly because the people loved him. Their opportunity came through one of Jesus' disciples, Judas, who volunteered to lead them to Jesus for a sum of money.

After eating the Passover meal with his disciples, Jesus went to the Mount of Olives to pray, as was his custom. Judas brought a crowd of men up on the mountain to arrest Jesus. They led him away to the high priest's house, and at dawn the religious leaders questioned him. "Are you the son of God?" they demanded.

"You are right in saying that I am," he replied. It was clear blasphemy according to Jewish law. They took him to Pilate, the governor appointed by Rome. Pilate decided that Jesus had not committed a crime worthy of death, but the religious leaders incited the crowd to demand Jesus' death. So Pilate handed Jesus over to them. They led him through the streets to a hill called The Skull. There Jesus lay down on a wooden cross. Stakes were put through his hands and feet to hold him to the cross. Then the cross was stood up in a hole in the ground, and the people waited for Jesus to die. Many women who had followed Jesus stood there watching.

It was the middle of the day, but the sky became dark for three hours. Then Jesus cried out loudly, "Father, into your hands I commit my spirit," and he died (Luke 23–24).

The cornerstone of the Christian faith is what happened with Jesus after his death. A member of the Jewish council who had opposed Jesus' crucifixion received permission to take the body off the cross. He wrapped it in linen cloth and placed it in a new tomb. The women who followed Jesus saw where the body was laid. They went to prepare spices and perfumes to anoint the body, but they could not return the next day because it was Sabbath and, according to Jewish law, they rested.

On the day after the Sabbath, early in the morning, the women went back to the tomb and found the stone rolled away from the entrance and no body inside. Two angels appeared to them and said, "Why do you look for the living among the dead? He is not here; he has risen" (Luke 24:5–6). The women ran back to tell the disciples what they had seen.

The Gospels describe several other appearances of Jesus to his disciples and followers after his resurrection.

JESUS' FINAL MESSAGE TO HIS FOLLOWERS

Jesus' final teachings focused on explaining his resurrection and encouraging his disciples to spread the message. He told them:

> This is what is written: The Christ will suffer and rise
> from the dead on the third day, and repentance and

> forgiveness of sins will be preached in his name to all
> nations, beginning at Jerusalem.
>
> —LUKE 24:46–47

Then Jesus promised to help his followers by sending them a visitation of power. Christians believe this is the Holy Spirit, who is described in Acts 2.

After this, Jesus was taken to heaven and did not appear to his followers again.

CONCLUSION

In five chapters you have just walked through the lives of Jesus and Muhammad side by side. You have experienced how they spent their time and pursued their goals. This gives you the framework that you will need to understand what they taught. Their teachings will be the subject of the second half of this book.

You will have the opportunity to compare their teachings on the following key topics:

- Their messages to the world
- Their teachings about each other
- Healing and miracles
- The meaning of holy war
- Love
- Prayer
- Women

Before these topical chapters, I have placed timelines that list that major events in Jesus' and Muhammad's lives. These time lines will help you review the biographies you just read and understand the teachings that follow.

9

Time Lines

MUHAMMAD TIME LINE

A.D. 570, *birth*

Muhammad was born in Mecca. (Islamic history says the specific day was Monday, the twelfth day of the first month [Rabir]. On the Christian calendar, this would be August 2.)

A.D. 576, *age 6*

Muhammad's mother died; his paternal grandfather assumed his care.

A.D. 578, *age 8*

Muhammad's grandfather died; his father's brother, Abu Talib, assumed his care.

A.D. 582, *age 12*

Muhammad's uncle Abu Talib took him to Syria where Bahira, a Nestorian Christian monk, prophesied over Muhammad.

A.D. 595, *age 25*

Married his first wife, Khadija, in a ceremony conducted by her cousin Waraqa, an Ebionite Christian priest.

A.D. 610, *age 40*

Reported the first revelation from the angel Gabriel.

A.D. 613, *age 43*

Started to preach openly in Mecca about his revelations.

A.D. 615, age 45

Muhammad sent eleven Muslims to Abysinnia (modern-day Ethiopia) to give them refuge from the persecution they were experiencing in Mecca. This is known as the first *hijra* (or pilgrimage).

Leaders of the Quraysh tribe boycotted the Muslims and Muhammad's clan, refusing to intermarry or sell them food. They lifted the boycott two or three years later.

A.D. 620, age 50

Reported the story of the Night Journey from Mecca to Jerusalem. During the same year both his first wife Khadija and his uncle and protector Abu Talib died.

A.D. 623, A.H. 1, age 53

Established a contract for the two strongest tribes of Medina to become his protectors.

Emigrated from Mecca to Medina (the second *hijra*). This marks the first year of the Islamic calendar. A.H. means "after *hijra.*"

Married his second wife, Aisha. (In the next ten years, he took eleven more women as wives.)

Received a revelation calling for *jihad*, or holy war, against nonbelievers for the first time.

Ordered his Uncle Hamza to go out with thirty Muslim soldiers to ambush a Quraysh caravan. It was the first time he ordered an attack.

Sent one of his cousins to attack idol worshipers from Mecca.

Sent a cousin (Saad ibn Abu Waqqas) to attack idol worshipers in Al-Kharrar.

A.D. 624, A.H. 2, age 54

This was a year of a great amount of jihad.

Many Jewish people in Medina claimed to convert to Islam.

Attack on Al-Abuwaa.

Battle of Badr. Muhammad personally led the Muslims in an attack against Mecca's army in the Valley of Badr. The Muslims won a surprising victory.

Attack on Beni Salib (idol worshipers).

Attack on al-Sawiq (idol worshipers).

Gave his daughter, Fatima, in marriage to his cousin Ali ibn abi Talib.

Sent out seven other raids (*suriya*) this year. (These are small raids of thirty to one hundred soldiers.)

A.D. 625, A.H. 3, *age 55*

Battle of Uhud. The Muslims suffered a defeat to the Meccans. (Muhammad's uncle Hamza was killed.)

Assassinated a Jewish leader named Kaab Ibn al-Ashraf, for speaking out against him. This shocked both Jews in Medina and idol worshipers in Mecca. It was the first time Muhammad used assassination.

Sent out three other raids (*suriya*) this year.

A.D. 626, A.H. 4, *age 56*

Attack on Beni Nadir (Jewish tribe).

Sent out two other raids (*suriya*) this year.

A.D. 627, A.H. 5, *age 57*

Raid on Dumatu'l-Jandel.

Battle of the Trench. People of Mecca and some Jews from Medina tried to attack the Muslims at Medina. The Muslims dug trenches around the city and the Meccans chose to go back without much of a fight.

Attack on the Jewish tribe of Beni Qurayzah, in which Muhammad killed all men and took the women and children as captives. This was punishment for their alleged involvement in the Battle of the Trench.

Assassination of another Jewish leader, Abi-Rafa.

Attack on Beni-Lihyan (Arab tribe).

Attack on Zi-kerd.

Attack on Beni al-Mustaliq (Jewish tribe). Muhammad's second wife, Aisha, was accused of having an affair during this raid.

A.D. 628, A.H. 6, age 58

Muhammad did not lead any battles this year, but he did send out a few raids (*suriya*).

A.D. 629, A.H. 7, age 59

Sent out five raids (*suriya*) this year.

Attack on Khaybar (Jewish village).

A.D. 630, A.H. 8, age 60

Raid on Mu'ta.

Battle of Zat-al-Salasil.

Invasion and conquest of Mecca.

Battle of Hunan.

Raid on Utas.

Raid on al-Ta-if.

A.D. 631, A.H. 9, age 61

This is called the Year of Submission. People from all over the area who hadn't been attacked yet sent messengers to Muhammad saying, "We submit to you." Islamic history names forty-eight different groups who sent this message to Muhammad. Muhammad started sending letters to leaders and kings of the cities and countries around him to ask them to convert to Islam.

Raid on Ta-buk.

A.D. 632, A.H. 9, age 62

Sent governors (*amirs*) to rule over the areas where people and tribes agreed to accept his prophethood.

A.D. 633, A.H. 10, age 63

Established the practice of *hajj*.

Preached final sermon, known as the Sermon on Mount Arafat.

A.D. 634, A.H. 11, age 64

Became ill with fever.

Died.

JESUS TIME LINE[1]

6/5 B.C.

Born in Bethlehem.

5/4 B.C.

Mary and Joseph took Jesus to Egypt to escape Herod's order to kill all male children under the age of two.

4/3 B.C., age 2

Mary and Joseph returned to their home in Nazareth.

A.D. 6/7, age 12

Stayed behind at the temple in Jerusalem after his family started to travel back home.

A.D. 26, age 32

John the Baptist began to teach publicly.

Ministry begins
A.D. 26/27, age 32 or 33

Jesus was baptized by John the Baptist and began to teach publicly.

Performed his first miracle—changing water to wine.

Drove money changers out of the temple in Jerusalem.

Spoke to the Samaritan woman at the well.

Healed an official's son.

Preached at the synagogue in his hometown of Nazareth and was rejected.

Second year of ministry

Healed a demon-possessed man in the synagogue at Capernaum.

Healed a leper.

Healed a paralyzed man.

Healed a crippled man at the Pool of Bethesda.

Healed a man with a shriveled hand.

Selected his twelve apostles and preached the Sermon on the Mount.

Healed a Roman centurion's servant.

Raised a widow's son from the dead.

Calmed a storm on the Sea of Galilee.

Healed a demon-possessed man living among graves.

Raised a girl from the dead and healed a woman of a bleeding problem.

Third year of ministry

Sent out the twelve apostles to preach his message.

Fed five thousand people with five loaves and two fish.

Healed the daughter of a Gentile woman.

Healed a deaf-mute man.

Fed four thousand people.

Healed a blind man.

Healed a boy with symptoms of epilepsy.

Healed ten lepers.

Forgave a woman caught in adultery.

Healed another blind man.

Raised Lazarus from the dead.

The final journey to Jerusalem
A.D. 30, age 35 or 36

Healed one or two blind men in Jericho.

Ate dinner with Lazarus, Mary, and Martha.

Entered Jerusalem surrounded by a happy crowd (Sunday before his death).

Ate the Last Supper with his disciples (Thursday before his death).

Arrested, put on trail, and crucified (Friday).

Resurrected from the dead and appeared to followers (Sunday after his death).

SECTION 3
THEIR LEGACY
IN WORDS AND DEEDS

10

Their Messages to the World

We've seen how Jesus and Muhammad spread their messages. Now we need to see exactly what these messages were. In this chapter you will learn:

· What they taught about their identity and purpose
· How they told people to please God
· How people could be pardoned for offenses against God
· What they taught about fate after death

WHO THEY CLAIMED TO BE
MUHAMMAD: THE FINAL PROPHET

Identity

Muhammad declared that he was the final prophet that Allah would send to the world. He explained:

> My similitude in comparison with the other Prophets before me is that of a man who has built a house nicely and beautifully, except for a place of one brick in a corner. The people go round about it and wonder at its beauty, but say: "Would that this brick be put in its place!" So I am that brick, and I am the last (end) of the Prophets.[1]

Muhammad said that he was the fulfillment of the prophecies of both the Old and New Testament about a prophet that would come. In other words, he claimed to be a prophet for whom both the Jews and Christians were waiting.

> Some of the friends of the apostle of Allah said to him,
> O apostle of Allah, tell us about yourself.
>
> He said, "Yes, I am the message of my father Abraham
> and the good news of my brother Jesus."[2]

Muhammad also taught that Jews and Christians had corrupted their Scriptures so that references to Muhammad's coming were taken out. Modern Islamic scholars have claimed to find references to Muhammad that are still remaining in the Bible. You can read more about this topic in Appendix B.

Though he said he was the final and greatest prophet, Muhammad also stated clearly that he was human, not divine. Muhammad told the people, "I am only a man like you" (Surah 18:110). He would die like any other human being. The Quran says, "Verily you (O Muhammad) will die, and verily they (too) will die" (Surah 39:30).

Regarding his relationship to Allah, the Quran describes Muhammad as a "slave" of Allah (Surah 2:23). Converts to Islam are described as "slaves" to Allah as well (Surah 50:8).

Purpose

In the beginning Muhammad said that Allah's purpose for him was to be a "plain warner" (Surah 71:2).

> But (you are sent) as a mercy from your Lord, to give warning to a people to whom no warner had come before you: in order that they may remember or receive admonition.
>
> —SURAH 28:46

However, after Muhammad moved to Medina, he became more than a warner: he became a conqueror. He said in his last sermon on the Mount of Arafat:

After today there will no longer be two religions existing in Arabia. I descended by Allah with the sword in my hand, and my wealth will come from the shadow of my sword. And the one who will disagree with me will be humiliated and persecuted.[3]

Muhammad called for idol worshipers to leave their idols and for Jews and Christians to leave their "corrupted" faiths and to accept Islam.

JESUS: THE SON OF GOD

Identity

Jesus stated many times in the Gospel records that he was the son of God or that God was his father. For example:

> [Jesus] asked [Peter]. "Who do you say I am?" Simon Peter answered, "You are the Christ, the Son of the living God." Jesus replied, "Blessed are you, Simon son of Jonah, for this was not revealed to you by man, but by my Father in heaven."
> —MATTHEW 16:15–17

> [Jesus said] Why then do you accuse me of blasphemy because I said, "I am God's Son"? Do not believe me unless I do what my Father does. But if I do it, even though you do not believe me, believe the miracles, that you may know and understand that the Father is in me, and I in the Father.
> —JOHN 10:36–38

> [The high priest said to Jesus] "I charge you under oath by the living God: Tell us if you are the Christ, the Son of God." "Yes, it is as you say," Jesus replied.
> —MATTHEW 26:63–64

(Other verses where Jesus referred to himself as the son of God include Matthew 4:6; 8:29; 10:32; 11:27; 16:15–17, 27; 27:43; 28:19; Mark 1:11; Luke 2:49; 10:22; John 3:16–18; 5:17–18, 25; 10:36; 11:4.)

Jesus said that he was the fulfillment of Jewish prophecy about a coming Messiah.

> Do not think that I have come to abolish the Law or the Prophets; I have not come to abolish them but to fulfill them.
>
> —MATTHEW 5:17

> This is what I told you while I was still with you: Everything must be fulfilled that is written about me in the Law of Moses, the Prophets and the Psalms.
>
> —LUKE 24:44

Jesus' words are supported by many Old Testament prophecies that were fulfilled in his life, such as being born in Bethlehem, living in Nazareth, spending time in Egypt, and details about his final days. Please see Appendix C for a more complete list, including references.

Purpose

The Old Testament Scriptures taught that God required an animal sacrifice to pardon offenses. Jesus said that his purpose was to offer himself as the final sacrifice for the offenses of every person.

> The Son of Man [came] to give his life as a ransom for many.
>
> —MARK 10:45 (SEE ALSO JOHN 3:14.)

Jesus asked people to believe his message so that they could have eternal life.

> For God so loved the world that he gave his one and only Son, that whoever believes in him shall not perish but have eternal life. For God did not send his Son into the world to condemn the world, but to save the world through him.
>
> —JOHN 3:16–17

HOW TO PLEASE GOD

The essence of any religion is how humanity can have a good relationship with God. The teachings of Jesus and Muhammad were very different in this area.

Requirements to be a Muslim

Muhammad's message developed and became clearer over his lifetime. In other words, the duties required of a Muslim were not the same in the beginning of the revelation as they were twenty-three years later at the end. For example, in Mecca during the early years, Muslims were not required to pray a specific number of times per day. After Muhammad's Night Journey, which occurred ten years after his first revelation, prayer was required five times a day. Another example is the pilgrimage to Mecca (*hajj*), which was not a requirement until Muhammad's ninth year in Medina.

We will look at his message in its final development. The requirements to be a Muslim were:

1. Worship Allah alone, accept Muhammad as Allah's prophet, and believe in the Quran.

2. Pray the Islamic ritual prayer at the five prescribed times per day. (In chapter 15, I will describe Islamic prayer in detail.)

3. Pay zakat (charity) to the "house of money," which Muhammad administered. Every person was required to give 2.5 percent of whatever kind of income he earned. The zakat was not an optional donation. Muhammad used the money to partly finance the Muslim military, support the poor, and pay for building projects. There was no word "tax" in that time, but this is really how the money functioned. There was no secular government, so the Islamic state did the only tax collection. In the present time, Muslims are living under secular

governments and must pay taxes to them. So the zakat is in addition to their secular taxes. Because there is no central Islamic state, each person must choose where to give his money.

4. Fast between first prayers and fourth prayers during the month of Ramadan.

5. Make a pilgrimage to Al-Ka'ba in Mecca (Surah 22:27).

In addition to these things, Muhammad in Medina exhorted the people that Allah "loved" those who would fight hard for him in the raids and battles that the Muslims conducted against the nonbelievers in Arabia (Surahs 8 and 9).

Requirements to please God

Jesus' message stayed the same from beginning to end. He said that he was the way to have a right relationship with God. "I am the way, the truth, and the life. No one comes to the Father except through me" (John 14:6).

Jesus did not have a list of requirements for his followers to meet. Instead, he simply invited them:

> "Come, follow me."
>
> —MARK 1:17

And they did follow him.

> "And a great crowd of people followed him."
>
> —JOHN 6:2

Yet Jesus did not say that following him would be easy. He warned that their lives would be in danger.

> Then he called the crowd to him along with his disciples and said: "If anyone would come after me, he must deny himself and take up his cross and follow me. For whoever wants to save his life will lose it, but whoever loses his life for me and for the gospel will save it.
>
> —MARK 8:34–35

But Jesus also promised that he would not burden his followers.

> Come to me, all you who are weary and burdened, and I will give you rest. Take my yoke upon you and learn from me, for I am gentle and humble in heart, and you will find rest for your souls. For my yoke is easy and my burden is light.
>
> —MATTHEW 11:28–30

He asked them to obey the two "greatest" commandments:

> On one occasion an expert in the law stood up to test Jesus. "Teacher," he asked, "what must I do to inherit eternal life?"
>
> "What is written in the Law?" he replied. "How do you read it?"
>
> He answered: "'Love the Lord your God with all your heart and with all your soul and with all your strength and with all your mind'; and, 'Love your neighbor as yourself.'"
>
> "You have answered correctly," Jesus replied. "Do this and you will live."
>
> —LUKE 10:25–28

In short, the requirements to be a Christian were to follow Jesus, love God, and love other people. In contrast to Muhammad, Jesus did not ask his disciples to follow laws about when to pray, how much money to give, how often to fast, or when to take a pilgrimage.

PARDON FOR OFFENSES

If you teach about how to please God, then you must also explain what happens when the inevitable mistakes are made. In other words, what are God's requirements for forgiveness? Let's see what Jesus and Muhammad said.

Allah decides whose sins will be forgiven

There is a well-known story in Islamic history about the death of Muhammad's uncle Abu Talib, who had protected Muhammad from his enemies in Mecca for many years. As his uncle lay dying, Muhammad begged him to confess Islam, but his uncle did not. Afterward Muhammad reported a revelation from Allah, which said:

> Whether you (O Muhammad) ask forgiveness for them (hypocrites) or ask not forgiveness for them—(and even) if you ask seventy times for their forgiveness— Allâh will not forgive them, because they have disbelieved in Allâh and His Messenger (Muhammad). And Allâh guides not those people who are *Fâsiqûn* (rebellious, disobedient to Allâh).
>
> —SURAH 9:80

In other words, Muhammad said he had no ability to forgive someone of wrongdoing or to convince Allah to forgive. Muhammad only said he was able to have his uncle's punishment reduced as follows:

> Among the inhabitants of the Fire Abu Talib would have the least suffering, and he would be wearing two shoes (of Fire) which would boil his brain.[4]

On a different occasion, Muhammad said he asked Allah to forgive his mother, who had died when Muhammad was only six. One of Muhammad's servants told the story this way:

> Abu Hariara narrated: "The prophet Muhammad visited the grave of his mother, and cried and cried and made all of us around him cry. Muhammad said, 'I asked Allah whether I can ask him to forgive my mother, and he said no but only he gave me permission to visit her grave.'"[5]

Again Muhammad declared that he could not influence Allah to forgive sins. Through the Quran and the hadith, Muhammad taught that only Allah had the authority to forgive sins.

All offenses were not equal in Islamic theology. There were great sins and little sins. Examples of great sins were worshiping another god besides Allah; denying any of the basic beliefs of Islam, especially the five pillars; insulting Muhammad; killing people outside the guidelines of Islamic law; and slandering another Muslim while he is not present. The offender must repent before Allah, but Allah decides whether or not to forgive him. On Judgment Day the person will discover whether or not Allah will forgive him.

On the other hand, little sins could be forgiven by doing good deeds, like extra prayer, extra fasting, or extra charity. Examples of small sins are missing prayer for a day, lying, eating during Ramadan fasting, or refusing to help a neighbor in need.

In short, Allah alone decides whether a person is forgiven. If he commits a big sin, he is at Allah's mercy. If he commits a little sin, he can earn forgiveness through good works or going on *hajj* (pilgrimage to Mecca).

Allah's forgiveness for those to fight

After Muhammad began sending out military expeditions from Medina, he received revelations about a special way Muslims could earn forgiveness from Allah—by fighting and dying for the cause of Islam. One revelation described fighting for Allah as a "trade." If you give Allah "your wealth and your lives" he will forgive your sins, admit you into paradise, and help you win your battle. Here is the passage from the Quran:

> O you who believe! Shall I guide you to a trade that will save you from a painful torment? That you believe in Allah and His Messenger (Muhammad), and that you strive hard and fight in the Cause of Allah with your wealth and your lives: that will be better for you, if you but know! (If you do so) He will *forgive you your sins*, and admit you into Gardens under which rivers flow, and pleasant dwellings in 'Adn (Eden) Paradise; that is indeed the great success. And also (He will give you)

> another (blessing) which you love,—help from Allah
> (against your enemies) and a near victory.
>
> —SURAH 61:10–13, EMPHASIS ADDED

Muslims further interpret this to mean that a person who dies in jihad goes straight to paradise and does not need to wait in his grave for Judgment Day.

What Jesus taught about forgiveness

While Muhammad said he had no ability to forgive sin, Jesus openly proclaimed that he had complete authority to forgive sin.

> Some men brought to him a paralytic, lying on a mat.
> When Jesus saw their faith, he said to the paralytic,
> "Take heart, son; your sins are forgiven." At this, some
> of the teachers of the law said to themselves, "This
> fellow is blaspheming!" Knowing their thoughts, Jesus
> said, "Why do you entertain evil thoughts in your hearts?
> Which is easier: to say, 'Your sins are forgiven,' or to say,
> 'Get up and walk'? But so that you may know that the
> Son of Man has authority on earth to forgive sins...."
> Then he said to the paralytic, "Get up, take your mat
> and go home." And the man got up and went home.
>
> —MATTHEW 9:2–7; SEE ALSO LUKE 7:36–50

When John the Baptist saw Jesus walking toward him, he exclaimed, "Look, the lamb of God who takes away the sin of the world" (John 1:29). When Jesus was speaking of his death by crucifixion, he said, "This is my blood of the covenant which is poured out for many for the forgiveness of sins" (Matt. 26:28).

In other words, Jesus not only claimed to have the ability to forgive sins on behalf of God while he was on earth, but he also claimed that his death would function as a substitute sacrifice, securing forgiveness for all humanity for all time. One of his final statements to his disciples was this:

> This is what is written: The Christ will suffer and rise
> from the dead on the third day, and repentance and

forgiveness of sins will be preached in his name to all
nations, beginning at Jerusalem.

—LUKE 24:46–47, EMPHASIS ADDED

FATE AFTER DEATH

We know what Jesus and Muhammad taught about themselves and
what they required their followers to do. Now let us compare their
teachings about how God or Allah treats people when they die.

A Muslim's fate after death

Muhammad taught that after death a person remains in his
grave until Judgment Day. If the person was good, his grave would
be a little paradise. If he was bad, it would be a place of torment
(Surah 55:46–60). However, nowhere did Muhammad reveal how
a person could know for sure whether he would have pleasure or
torment in the grave.

As a Muslim, I was personally frustrated by this lack of information. I wondered, "Why would the god of the Quran reveal so
many guidelines about earthly matters, like what to do during a
woman's period, but fail to reveal how I can know whether I will
be tortured or comforted when I die?"

Muhammad himself expressed concern about what would
happen to him in his grave. His wife Aisha reported:

> Two old Jewish women visited me in my house and
> said to me, "The dead in their graves are punished." I
> didn't believe them. After they left I went to prophet
> Muhammad and told him and he said, "Yes, they told
> you the truth; that some dead people are punished
> and even animals can hear their cries in the grave."
> From that day, every time I saw the prophet pray, he
> asked Allah to rescue him from the punishment of
> the grave.[6]

Muhammad taught that Judgment Day would be announced by
the sound of a trumpet. Both the dead and the living would come
together, driven by angels to the judgment square to be judged by

Allah himself. Allah would weigh their good and bad deeds and decide who would go to paradise and who would go to hell. Until Judgment Day, a person cannot know whether he has pleased Allah. (See Surah 6:73ff, 18:99ff, 20:102ff, 23:101ff, 27:87ff, 36:48ff, 39:68ff, 50:20ff, 78:18ff.)

Muhammad himself said that he did not know what would happen to him at Judgment Day. Let's look at when he made this statement. Muhammad was visiting a home where a Muslim man had died and the body was still there. A woman said to the dead body, "May Allah's mercy be on you. I testify that Allah has honored you."

Muhammad said to the woman, "How do you know that [Allah honored the man]?"

She answered, "I do not know, by Allah."

Muhammad replied: "As for him, death has come to him and I wish him all good from Allah. By Allah, though I am Allah's apostle, I neither know what will happen to me, nor do you."[7]

Muhammad's loyal follower Abu Bakr also spoke of fearing Allah's judgment. He said, "If one of my feet were inside paradise, and the other one were still out, I would not yet trust the cunning of Allah."[8] Bakr meant that his eternal fate was a mystery until both feet were inside paradise.

Abu Bakr was nicknamed the "crying man" because he would continually cry as he prayed.[9] When asked about this one time his answer was, "Every time I start to pray I imagine Allah standing in front of me and the king of death behind me, the paradise to my right and hell to my left side, and I do not know what my God is going to do to me."[10]

Muhammad's teachings gave Muslims little comfort when a loved one died.

> Muhammad saw a woman crying at the grave of her son. He said, "Be a good believer and be patient." The woman said, "Go away because you have not lost a loved one like me." She did not recognize him.[11]

Let's examine Muhammad's words of comfort to this woman. He told her to be a good Muslim and be patient. In Islamic teaching, the woman's son was under the will of Allah. Nobody knows if he will go to paradise or hell; Allah decides. So Muhammad was telling the woman to accept Allah's decision, whatever it was. This wasn't very comforting to her.

Destiny

Muhammad's teaching on Judgment Day works in combination with his teaching on destiny. The result is great uncertainty in the minds of Muslims regarding their fates after death:

> Allah's Apostle, the true and truly inspired said, "(As regards your creation), every one of you is collected in the womb of his mother for the first forty days, and then he becomes a clot for another forty days, and then a piece of flesh for another forty days. Then Allah sends an angel to write four words: He writes his deeds, time of his death, means of his livelihood, and whether he will be wretched or blessed (in religion). Then the soul is breathed into his body. So a man may do deeds characteristic of the people of the (Hell) Fire, so much so that there is only the distance of a cubit between him and it, and then what has been written (by the angel) surpasses, and so he starts doing deeds characteristic of the people of Paradise and enters Paradise. Similarly, a person may do deeds characteristic of the people of Paradise, so much so that there is only the distance of a cubit between him and it, and then what has been written (by the angel) surpasses, and he starts doing deeds of the people of the (Hell) Fire and enters the (Hell) Fire."[12]

Let me summarize what this hadith says so that you can understand it easily. Muhammad taught that when a person is still in his mother's womb, Allah sends an angel to write down four facts about this person's life: (1) his deeds, (2) his time of death,

(3) his means of livelihood, and (4) whether he will be wretched or blessed (meaning whether he will go to hell or paradise).

Therefore, a person may do evil deeds all his life. But, if while he was in his mother's womb the angel wrote that he will be "blessed," then at the end of his life this destiny will take over and he will start doing good deeds and end up in paradise. The reverse is also true: a person may do good deeds all his life, but if the angel wrote that he will be "wretched," then at the end of his life this destiny will take over and the person will start doing evil deeds and end up in hell.

How does this apply to daily life? If you are a Muslim, you hope that Allah will accept your good deeds and admit you into paradise. But because you are taught that your final destiny is based on a word that an angel wrote before you were born, your hope is always shadowed by doubt. *What if I am one of those who was destined for good deeds during my life but ultimately sentenced to hell?*

Jesus' teaching on fate after death

Judgment Day was also a part of Jesus' teachings (Matt. 10:15, 11:22–24, 12:36, 41–42, 24:31; Luke 10:14, 11:31–32). Regarding Judgment Day, Jesus said:

- No one but God knows the date (Matt. 24:36).
- A trumpet will sound (Matt. 24:31).
- Angels will gather the people (Matt. 13:41).

As you just read, Muhammad described these same details six hundred years later. (See Surah 6:73ff, 18:99ff, 20:102ff, 23:101ff, 27:87ff, 36:48ff, 39:68ff, 50:20ff, 78:18ff.) However, Jesus' teaching on Judgment Day differed from Muhammad's in important ways. For example, Jesus said he would return and do the judging (Matt. 13:24–30, 36–41, 47–50; 25:31–33; John 5:22). Muhammad said Allah would be the judge.

Jesus told four parables in Matthew 24 and 25 about Judgment Day, describing the criteria by which people would be judged.

Each parable calls for people to love God and love their neighbors in order to receive eternal life.

Does this mean that Jesus requires good works in order for a person to enter heaven? This is an important question that we can answer through the teachings of Jesus himself. Jesus said that faith in him is required for everlasting life: "God gave his one and only Son so that whoever believes in him shall not perish but have eternal life" (John 3:16). And Jesus also said, "If you love me, you will obey what I command" (John 14:15). This means that if you truly believe Jesus is the son of God, you will obey his commands. If you do not obey his commands, then you do not believe in him.

This understanding is supported by the writings of Jesus' followers. James, one of Jesus' three closest disciples, wrote, "Faith without deeds is dead" (James 2:26). He described good works as proof of faith: "I will show you my faith by what I do" (James 2:18). The Book of Ephesians states simply: "For it is by grace you have been saved, through faith—and this not from yourselves, it is the gift of God—not by works, so that no one can boast" (Eph. 2:8–9).

Therefore, on Judgment Day, Jesus will look for good works as evidence of faith in him.

Regarding what happens to the dead as they wait for Judgment Day, Jesus gave very little teaching. However, he did describe a scene where a rich man died and went to Hades and a poor man died and went to "Abraham's side," which was a place of comfort (Luke 16:19–31). This gives us an indication of where people who have died will wait until Judgment Day. Other details about judgments for believers and unbelievers are described in other parts of the New Testament, especially the Book of Revelation.

CONCLUSION

Jesus and Muhammad had profoundly different ideas about pleasing God, forgiveness, and Judgment Day. They also saw their roles as messengers of God in different ways as well. In the next chapter we will look at what Muhammad said about Jesus and what Jesus might have said about Muhammad.

11

Their Teachings About
Each Other

M ost westerners would be surprised to know that Muhammad
and the Quran expressed great respect for Jesus. The first
half of this chapter will look at the many teachings Muhammad
gave about Jesus. Jesus, however, never spoke directly about
Muhammad because Jesus lived almost six hundred years before
Muhammad was born. Even so, I believe we can make an educated
guess about what Jesus *might have said* about Muhammad, based
on the teachings of Jesus that we already know. The second half of
this chapter will present these ideas.

MUHAMMAD'S RESPECT FOR JESUS

Muhammad described himself and Jesus as "brothers in the faith."

> Allah's Messenger said: I am most close to Jesus, son
> of Mary, among the whole of mankind in this worldly
> life and the next life. They said: Allah's Messenger
> how is it? Thereupon he said: Prophets are brothers
> in faith, having different mothers. Their religion is,
> however, one and there is no Apostle between us
> (between I and Jesus Christ).[1]

So Muhammad stated that he and Jesus practiced the same
religion. How can this be? In order to understand this and
Muhammad's other teachings about Jesus, you need to be aware
of how Muhammad described the relationship between Islam,
Christianity, and Judaism.

Islam, Judaism, and Christianity

Remember that Muhammad lived in a society that included Jews, Christians, and idol worshipers. Because Muhammad proclaimed one God only, as did the Jews and Christians, he needed to explain if this one God was the same as their one God.

His explanation was that Islam came first, and that Abraham practiced Islam before Christianity or Judaism was founded.

> Ibrahim (Abraham) was neither a Jew nor a Christian, but he was a true Muslim....Verily, among mankind who have the best claim to Ibrahim (Abraham) are those who followed him, and this Prophet (Muhammad) and those who have believed (Muslims).
>
> —SURAH 3:67–68

According to Muhammad, because Abraham practiced Islam and worshiped Allah, all the prophets that descended from him also practiced Islam. The Quran lists many of these biblical prophets by name including Isaac, Ishmael, Jacob, Joseph, Noah, David, Solomon, and Moses. In fact, the Quran even says John (the Baptist) and Jesus were prophets of Allah as well (Surah 4:163; 6:84–86; see also 2:130, 135; 3:95; 4:125; 6:161). Muhammad refers to all the prophets as his "brothers," except for referring to Abraham as father.

The question is: If all these prophets were following Islam, where did Judaism and Christianity come from? The Quran teaches that Jews and Christians distorted the messages of the prophets, and the result was Judaism and Christianity (Surah 2:75; cf. verses 76–79; Surah 5:13). Therefore, Jewish and Christian Scriptures are invalid.

Muhammad said that his revelations canceled out Christianity and Judaism and brought people back to the one true religion that Abraham understood and practiced (Islam).

Therefore, when Muhammad spoke of Jesus, he referred to him as a prophet of Allah who taught Islam.

Let's look at some of Muhammad's specific teachings about Jesus. We'll see that he agreed with the Bible regarding some events in Jesus' life. But Muhammad also contradicted the Bible's most significant teachings.

MUHAMMAD'S TEACHINGS ABOUT JESUS

Muhammad made many positive declarations about Jesus, particularly through Quranic revelation. I have prepared a complete list of verses in the Quran that describe attributes of Jesus that are mentioned in the Bible. Please read this list in Appendix D.

One of the most significant passages is Surah 3:33–63. Islamic scholars say that Muhammad presented these verses when he was visited in A.H. 9 by ten Christian bishops from Najran, an area near the northern border of modern Yemen. The bishops came to talk with Muhammad about Islam.

Muhammad said to them, "Be Muslims."

They said, "We are Muslims," meaning, "Even before we met you, we were worshiping one God only." So Muhammad went on to describe for them the differences between Islam and Christianity. First he presented stories about the birth of Mary, the mother of Jesus, and the birth of John the Baptist. (These stories included biblical details but also included much information not found in the Bible.) Then he described Jesus this way:

Jesus was born of a virgin.

> (Remember) when the angels said: "O Maryam (Mary)! Verily, Allah gives you the glad tidings of a Word...from Him, his name will be the Messiah Isa (Jesus), the son of Maryam (Mary), held in honour in this world and in the Hereafter, and will be one of those who are near to Allah....She said: "O my Lord! How shall I have a son when no man has touched me?" He said: "So (it will be) for Allah creates what He wills. When He has decreed something, He says to it only: "Be!"—and it is.
> —SURAH 3:45, 47; SEE ALSO 4:171

Muhammad not only affirmed before the Christians of Najran that Mary became pregnant as a virgin, but he also said that Jesus was the Messiah. Muhammad went on to affirm that Jesus performed miracles.

Jesus performed miracles.

> And will make him [Isa (Jesus)] a Messenger to the Children of Israel (saying): "I have come to you with a sign from your Lord, that I design for you out of clay, a figure of a bird, and breathe into it, and it becomes a bird by Allah's Leave; and I heal him who was born blind, and the leper, and I bring the dead to life by Allah's Leave."
>
> —SURAH 3:49

Although the story of the clay bird is not in the Gospels, the end of the verse bears a surprising resemblance to words of Jesus recorded in the Book of Matthew:

> Jesus replied, "Go back and report to John what you hear and see: The blind receive sight, the lame walk, those who have leprosy are cured, the deaf hear, the dead are raised, and the good news is preached to the poor.
>
> —MATTHEW 11:4–5

In other words, Muhammad agreed with Christians that Jesus performed great miracles, even raising people from the dead. (This is just a small part of the many positive references in the Quran to Jesus. Please see Appendix D for a complete list.) However, Muhammad differed from the biblical record in many ways. For example, he told this group of Christian bishops that Jesus worshiped Allah.

Jesus worshiped Allah.

> Truly! Allah is my Lord and your Lord, so worship Him (Alone). This is the Straight Path.[2]
>
> —SURAH 3:51

Muhammad said Jesus' disciples declared: We are Muslims (v. 52) and refused to worship anyone but Allah (v. 53). In other words, Muhammad said that the disciples refused to worship Jesus as God. However, the Gospels mention several examples of the disciples worshiping Jesus (Matt. 14:33; 28:9; Luke 24:51–52).

Muhammad concluded by telling his Christian visitors, "This is the true narrative…" (Surah 3:62). However, the delegation rejected Muhammad's message.

While Muhammad's speech to the bishops gives a good overview, let's look at several other statements in the Quran that show Muhammad's perspective on Jesus.

Muhammad said Jesus prophesied of his coming.

> And (remember) when Isa (Jesus), son of Maryam (Mary), said: "O Children of Israel! I am the Messenger of Allah unto you confirming the Taurat [(Torah) which came] before me, and giving glad tidings of a Messenger to come after me, whose name shall be Ahmad.
>
> —SURAH 61:6

Ahmad is one of the names of Muhammad, so Muhammad taught that Jesus prophesied of his coming. However, Muhammad also said that Christians had removed most of these references out of their Scriptures. Modern Muslim scholars have claimed that some of Jesus' sayings in the Book of John speak of Muhammad, however, Christians interpret these verses consistently to be references to the Holy Spirit (John 14:16–17, 24; 16:7; see also Appendix D).

God has no son.

A Christian who reads through the Quran would be surprised to see how often and specifically the Quran denies that God could have a son. For example:

> No son (or offspring) did Allah beget, nor is there any *ilah* (god) along with Him.
>
> —SURAH 23:91

> Say [O Muhammad]: "If (Allah) Most Gracious had a
> son, I would be the first to worship."
> —SURAH 43:81, ALI TRANSLATION

> Say not: "Three (trinity)!" Cease! (it is) better for
> you. For Allah is (the only) One *Ilah* (God), Glory be to
> Him (Far Exalted is He) above having a son.[3]
> —SURAH 4:171

Jesus should not be worshiped.

According to the Quran, Allah will ask Jesus on the Day of Resurrection, "Did you say unto men, 'Worship me and my mother as two gods besides Allah?'"

Jesus will reply, "Never did I say to them aught except what You (Allah) did command me to say, 'Worship Allah, my Lord and your Lord'" (Surah 5:116–117; see also v. 72).

Muhammad said that Christians were wrong to worship Jesus.

> I heard the Prophet saying, "Do not exaggerate in
> praising me as the Christians praised the son of Mary,
> for I am only a Slave. So, call me the Slave of Allah and
> His Apostle."[4]

Jesus did not rise from the dead.

Speaking of those who said they crucified Jesus, Muhammad stated:

> They killed him not, nor crucified him, but it appeared
> so to them....For surely; they killed him not....But
> Allah raised him up unto Himself.
> —SURAH 4:157–158

In other words, Muhammad said that instead of being crucified, Jesus was taken up directly to Allah.

CONCLUSION

Muhammad's teachings about Jesus, especially those from the Quran, were constantly positive and affirmed some of the biblical record. However, the Quranic revelation also repeatedly denied one of the most important claims that Jesus made: that he was the son of God. The Nestorian and Ebionite cults in Arabia during Muhammad's time also affirmed Jesus' prophethood while denying his divinity. Islam claimed Jesus as one of its prophets, and Muhammad declared that Jesus prophesied of his coming.

Now, let us think about what Jesus would have said about Muhammad.

JESUS' TEACHING ABOUT MUHAMMAD

Let me state from the beginning that this section about Jesus can only be written as an opinion. Jesus did not teach about Muhammad directly because he lived six hundred years before Muhammad. Therefore, we must apply what we know of Jesus' teachings to what we know about Muhammad. It is my opinion that Jesus would have challenged Muhammad's prophethood in three areas: (1) Muhammad's treatment of other people, (2) Muhammad's description of the requirements to please God, (3) Muhammad's description of the nature of God.

Treatment of other people

Jesus taught the crowds: "Watch out for false prophets....By their fruit you will recognize them....Every good tree bears good fruit, but a bad tree bears bad fruit" (Matt. 7:15–17).

The fruits of a person's life are his actions, so let us consider Muhammad's fruits. Through skillful warfare, debate, and intimidation, Muhammad had submitted all of Arabia to Islamic authority. In the process, his military killed thousands of people. Muhammad and his army had taken their wealth and sold their women and children into slavery.

You can argue that Muhammad was fighting for his survival and the survival of Islam. However, that argument holds up for only a short while. As he gained power, Muhammad began to aggressively pursue people who posed no threat to him at all.

As one who studied Islamic history in depth, I cannot avoid the facts of Muhammad's life. Muhammad's life reminds me of Jesus' description of the thief who comes to the sheepfold. "The thief comes only to steal and kill and destroy" (John 10:10). This was the fruit of Muhammad's life.

Judging by this standard, I believe if Jesus had encountered Muhammad, he would have called him a false prophet.

Requirements to please God

Both the Gospels of Matthew and Luke record Jesus' strong words of rebuke for the teachers of the law and chief priests. One of Jesus' complaints was that they burdened people with law without bringing them closer to God.

Jesus called them "blind guides." Why were they blind guides?

> And you experts in the law, woe to you, because you
> load people down with burdens they can hardly carry.
> —LUKE 11:46

The experts of the law required people to follow difficult rules for daily life and worship. In the same way, Muhammad required people to follow stringent Islamic laws (fast, pay the alm tax, pray five times a day, take a pilgrimage to Mecca, keep other Islamic laws) in order to please Allah.

The laws put a heavy burden on people and focused on the outward actions. Jesus challenged those who focused on laws. "You...clean the outside of the cup and dish, but inside you are full of greed and wickedness" (Luke 11:39). Jesus cried out against pious Jewish leaders who made a show of their long prayers while they repossessed widows' houses.

I believe Jesus would issue the same challenge to Muhammad, who taught Muslims to wash themselves on the outside five times a day before prayers, but at the same time he called for them to fight all the people of Arabia and used their greed for the spoils of war to motivate them to risk their lives. (See also Matthew 15.)

Jesus said the mercy of God was more powerful than the law. He rebuked the religious leaders for following the law and forgetting the mercy of God. For example, Jesus broke Jewish law by "working" on the Sabbath to heal a crippled woman (Luke 13:10–17).

I believe Jesus would have rebuked Muhammad for focusing on false requirements for pleasing God.

The nature of God

I believe Jesus would say to Muhammad, "Who is your Allah? The god you describe is totally different from the one I know." The Quran says the god of Islam works with Satan and demons to lead people astray (Surah 6:39, 126; 43:36–37). The Bible says God loves the world and does not want anyone to be led astray (John 3:16–17).

Jesus described a God of love; Muhammad (through Quranic revelation) described a God of punishment. If you do a search in the New Testament for the words *punishment/punish/punished*, you will come up with about 15 examples regarding unbelievers being punished in hell. (The Old Testament has 159 examples of these words.)

However, if you do a search in the Quran (which is a little shorter than the New Testament) for *punishment/punish/ punished*, you get 379 examples.[5] These verses describe how Allah punishes different types of people and sin.

You can also search for the word *love* in the Quran and find 82 examples. That's a pretty good number. But if you randomly check the context, you find repeated descriptions of what Allah does NOT love. (Chapter 14 explains more about the teachings of the Quran regarding love.)

If you do a computer search for the word *love* in the New Testament, you will get 260 verses. About one-third of these verses speak of God's love for his son or for people. About half describe people loving God or each other. And the remaining verses use the word *love* in the context of teaching, for example, "the love of money is a root of all kinds of evil" (1 Tim. 6:10).

Only one verse speaks of God *not* loving someone or something (Rom. 9:13).

Of course, one can simply conclude that the concept of love was used more in Jesus' society than Muhammad's society. But beyond that, these statistics point to a surprising difference between the nature of the God described by Muhammad and the God described by Jesus.

I believe Jesus would have challenged Muhammad's description of God.

Jesus' response to demons

Finally, let's look at a little-known story from Muhammad's life that demonstrated his humanity. In Christianity, it is a tremendous insult to say that a person of faith experienced demonic influence. But the Islamic point of view is different. It is not considered a failing of faith for a Muslim to experience demonic influence. In fact, according to a story in the hadith, Muhammad told Aisha that he was troubled by a "spell."

> A'isha reported that a Jew from among the Jews of Banu Zuraiq who was called Labid b. al-A'sam cast a spell upon Allah's Messenger with the result that he (under the influence of the spell) felt that he had been doing something whereas in fact he had not been doing that. (This state of affairs lasted) until one day or during one night Allah's Messenger made supplication (to dispel its effects). He again made a supplication and he again did this.[6]

This prompted the revelation of Surah 7:200.

> And if an evil whisper comes to you from *Shaitan* (Satan), then seek refuge with Allah.

If Muhammad were truly troubled by demons and he came to Jesus for help, we can guess what Jesus would have done. Jesus would have cast out the demons, as he had done for many others.

CONCLUSION

Jesus warned that false prophets would come, and he told his followers to identify them by whether their actions were good or evil. When Jesus encountered religious leaders who oppressed people, he rebuked them. I believe this information gives us an idea of how Jesus would have responded directly to Muhammad.

Now we have looked at what Jesus and Muhammad taught, who each claimed to be, and what they would have said about each other. Let's turn now to a specific teaching subject, in particular, healings and miracles.

12

Healings and Miracles

As a teenager, I had a great deal of respect in my community due to memorizing the Quran and attending Al-Azhar high school. As a result, people often called upon me to pray for friends or relatives who were sick.

When I visited someone who was sick, the first thing I would always do is sit next to him or her and recite from the Quran. I always recited the most well-known verse concerning healing:

> And if Allah touches you with harm, there is none who can remove it but He, and if He intends any good for you, there is none who can repel His Favour which He causes it to reach whomsoever of His slaves He wills.
> —SURAH 10:107

By reciting from the Quran, I hoped to get Allah's attention. Then I prayed: "O Allah, your slave is sick. Sickness comes from you, but healing also comes from you. So we ask your mercy."

I was always a little bit uncomfortable with doing this. I felt that Allah was very far away, and I did not know whether he would pay attention to me or not. After all, the Quran says that no one can intervene to change Allah's intentions:

> Say [O Muhammad]: "Who then has any power at all (to intervene) on your behalf with Allah, if He intends you hurt or intends you benefit?"
> —SURAH 48:11

Muhammad himself said that he was unable to influence Allah on his own behalf:

> Say (O Muhammad): I have no power over any harm
> or profit to myself except what Allah may will.
> —SURAH 10:49 (SEE ALSO SURAH 7:188.)

So I left the patient each time with no knowledge of whether Allah would acknowledge my prayer. But I had done what Allah allowed me to do.

Healing and miracles is an area where the differences between Jesus and Muhammad are most evident. Before beginning the comparison between Jesus and Muhammad, I would like to explain why this topic is an area of great debate among Muslims.

THE DEBATE ABOUT
MUHAMMAD AND MIRACLES

Whether Muhammad performed healings and miracles is a controversial topic among Muslims. Muslims accept that *Jesus* performed miracles (as supported by the Quran), but not everyone agrees on whether Muhammad performed miracles. This is because of contradictions between the Quran and the hadith (the record of Muhammad's teachings and actions). Remember that Muhammad had direct knowledge of what went into the Quran because the Quran is made up strictly of the revelations that he reported from the angel Gabriel. However, Muhammad did not have control over hadith. His followers could tell any story they wanted, whether it was true or not, and Muhammad had no control over it.

The Quran says Muhammad had no obligation to produce a sign to show that he was a prophet. Instead, the Quran is presented as the greatest sign of prophethood. Muhammad was to tell people:

> "The signs are only with Allah, and I am only a plain
> warner." Is it not sufficient for them that We[1] have

sent down to you the Book (the Quran) which is
recited to them?

—SURAH 29:50–51

In other words, Muhammad was to say, "I'm the prophet.
Don't ask me for signs. Signs are for Allah to do." The revelation
concluded, "The Quran is sign enough for you!"

All Muslims agree that the Quran is the greatest miracle given to
humanity. The Quran declares that no other human or spirit could
create a book to equal it.

Say: "If the mankind and the jinn were together to
produce the like of this Quran, they could nor produce
the like thereof, even if they helped one another."

—SURAH 17:88

Had We* sent down this Quran on a mountain, you
would surely have seen it humbling itself and rent
asunder by the fear of Allah.

—SURAH 59:21

That is why reports of miracles in the hadith raise suspicions
regarding their authenticity. Some Muslim scholars believe that most
of these miracle stories were invented by Muhammad's followers
after his death to help convince people that Muhammad was a true
prophet. Other Muslims, however, strongly believe that the miracle
accounts are accurate. When I was a child, I believed the stories I was
taught. But we weren't really taught much about Muhammad doing
miracles. This topic isn't emphasized in Islamic teaching.

With this understanding, let's compare the record regarding
miracles for Jesus and Muhammad. For clarity we will divide the
miracles into three categories: healing of physical illness, casting
out demons, and miracles in the natural world. Lastly, we will look
at whether Jesus or Muhammad empowered their followers to
perform healings or miracles.

---

*This use of the pronoun *We* in the Quran refers to Allah. Unlike in English,
where *we* indicates plurality, the usage in Arabic indicates greatness.

HEALING OF PHYSICAL ILLNESS

Muhammad

Even in the hadith, there are almost no stories about Muhammad praying for people to be healed of physical illness. I am only aware of the following two accounts.

Muhammad and Abu Bakr hid in a cave during their escape from Mecca to Medina (the second *hijra*). One historian says that Abu Bakr was bit by a poisonous snake and began to suffer from its poison. Muhammad said, "Don't be sad, Abu Bakr, because Allah is with us." Then Abu Bakr recovered.[2] This is a very popular story among Muslims and is often used in sermons, especially at the annual celebration of *hijra*. The story was said to be narrated by Umar ibn al-Khattib based on hearing it from Abu Bakr. Even the historian, Ibn Kathir, said that this hadith was not familiar to him and he was suspicious of its authenticity.

Ibn Kathir also mentioned a different version of the story. In this account, Abu Bakr was with the apostle of Allah in the cave, and Abu Bakr's hand was hurt by a stone. Muhammad did not try to pray for him or touch his hand for healing, but Abu Bakr created a one-line Arabic poem, addressed to his finger. "You are just a finger, you are just a bleeding finger, and this bleeding is just because of Allah." Ibn Kathir denied the story with the snake, but he said that the story of Abu Bakr hurting his finger was likely to be true. Despite the words of the historian, most Muslims still believe the story about the snake.

The second example of healing comes from a hadith narrated by Aisha, who was Muhammad's second wife. She said that Muhammad used to pray for healing for his wives and other sick Muslims, touching them with his right hand as he prayed.[3] However, Aisha is the only person who ever gave this report about Muhammad. If Muhammad commonly prayed for sick Muslims, then other followers should have reported it as well. There are no reports of people being healed after Muhammad's prayers.

Even if we find an account of healing in the hadith, it would stand directly against the teaching of the Quran, which says that Muhammad would not perform signs. If a hadith contradicts the Quran, the hadith must be rejected.

These comments of Aisha are usually not preached because healing is not a subject that the imams often discuss. It's just not a big part of Islam.

Rather than present examples of Allah providing healing, Islamic history shows some examples of times that healing was needed and it did *not* occur.

When the Muslims first came to Medina, many of them became sick and delirious from a high fever although Muhammad did not become sick. There is no record that he prayed for healings, but when he saw some Muslims doing their prayers while sitting down, he told them, "Know that the prayer of the sitter is only half as valuable as the prayer of the stander." The historian concludes: "Thereupon the Muslims painfully struggled to their feet despite their weakness and sickness, seeking a blessing."[4]

Muhammad had only two sons (Al-Kasim and Ibrahim), and both of them died in childhood. The hadith record this account of Ibrahim's death:

> We went with Allah's Apostle to the blacksmith Abu Saif, and he was the husband of the wet-nurse of Ibrahim (the son of the Prophet). Allah's Apostle took Ibrahim and kissed him and smelled him and later we entered Abu Saif's house and at that time Ibrahim was in his last breaths, and the eyes of Allah's Apostle started shedding tears. 'Abdur Rahman bin 'Auf said, "O Allah's Apostle, even you are weeping!" He said, "O Ibn 'Auf, this is mercy." Then he wept more and said, "The eyes are shedding tears and the heart is grieved, and we will not say except what pleases our Lord, O Ibrahim! Indeed we are grieved by your separation."[5]

If Muhammad could pray for healing, I believe he would have done so to keep his son from dying.

So the record is pretty simple: prayer for healing was not a significant part of Muhammad's life. It is possible that he never prayed for healings.

Jesus

If you have read through any of the Gospels, you will notice that accounts of physical healing make up a significant part of the story line. Examples of healings include:

- An official's son who was dying (John 4:48–52)

- Fever of Peter's mother-in-law (Matt. 8:14–15; Mark 1: 29–31; Luke 4:38–39)

- Men with leprosy (This disfiguring skin disease was often fatal.) (Matt. 8:1–4; Mark 1:40–45; Luke 5: 12–19; 17:11–19)

- Paralyzed man (Matt. 9:1–8; Mark 2:1–12; Luke 5: 18–26)

- Invalid at the Pool of Bethesda (John 5:1–15)

- A man with a shriveled hand (Matt. 12:9–13; Mark 3: 1–6; Luke 6:6–11)

- Roman army officer's sick servant (Matt. 8:5–13; Luke 7:2–10)

- Raised widow's son from the dead (Luke 7:11–17)

- Raised a ruler's daughter from the dead (Matt. 9: 18–26; Mark 5:21–43; Luke 8:40–56)

- Woman with menstrual problem (Matt. 9:20–22; Mark 5:24–34; Luke 8:43–48)

- Blind men (Matt. 9:32–34; 20:29–34; Mark 8:22–25; 10:46–52; John 9:1–38; 18:35–43)

- A man who was deaf and unable to talk (Mark 7:31–37)

- A woman who was bent over and crippled (Luke 13:10–17)

- A man with dropsy (or edema) (Luke 14:1–6)

- Raised his friend Lazarus from the dead out of his grave (John 11:1–44)

- Restored the ear of the high priest's servant after Peter struck him with a sword (Luke 22:49–51)

Regarding healing, we can see some ironic comparisons between Jesus and Muhammad. For example, Muhammad did not help his followers who were suffering from a fever, but the Gospels specifically mentioned Jesus healing fevers for two people—Peter's mother-in-law (Mark 1:29–31) and the official's son (John 4:48–52). Also, though Muhammad could not save his two sons from death, Jesus raised two children from the dead—a ruler's daughter and a widow's son. Jesus also healed a boy who was close to death in Capernaum just by telling his father, "Your son will live" (John 4:50).

At this point, we have established that healings played a major role in Jesus' life and a minor, or nonexistent, role in Muhammad's life. Now let's see what Jesus and Muhammad taught about the purpose of healing and the causes of sickness.

PURPOSE OF HEALINGS AND THE CAUSES OF SICKNESSES

Muhammad

I know of no teaching from Muhammad regarding the purpose of healing. He did, however, teach about the source of illness. Let's look again at the verse that I would quote to people who were sick:

And if Allah touches you with harm, there is none who
can remove it but He, and if He intends any good for
you, there is none who can repel His Favour which He
causes it to reach whomsoever of His slaves He wills.

—Surah 10:107

Muhammad taught that sickness came from Allah, so Muslims
believe that when a person is affected by sickness, there is a
reason behind it. Maybe the sick person did something wrong
or sinned against Allah, so Allah gave him a disease to purify
him from his wrongdoing. Muslims believe this purification will
put that person in a better position to stand in front of Allah on
Judgment Day.

This verse also says that Allah is the only one who can remove
the disease. This teaching frustrated me as a Muslim. I wondered,
"If you are sick and you pray to Allah for help, what do you expect?
If Allah is the one who sent the disease, how can you convince him
to take it back?"

Jesus

Jesus said that his healings and miracles were a sign to show
people that he really came from God.

When John heard in prison what Christ was doing, he
sent his disciples to ask him, "Are you the one who
was to come, or should we expect someone else?"
Jesus replied, "Go back and report to John what you
hear and see: The blind receive sight, the lame walk,
those who have leprosy are cured, the deaf hear, the
dead are raised, and the good news is preached to the
poor.

—Matthew 11:2–5

Similarly, Jesus said to the Jews:

The Jews gathered around him, saying, "How long
will you keep us in suspense? If you are the Christ, tell
us plainly." Jesus answered, "I did tell you, but you do

not believe. The miracles I do in my Father's name speak for me.

—JOHN 10:24–25

The Gospels also say Jesus was motivated to heal out of compassion for the people's suffering.

When Jesus landed and saw a large crowd, he had compassion on them and healed their sick.

—MATTHEW 14:14;
SEE ALSO MATTHEW 20:34; MARK 1:41

Jesus' compassion for people's sickness is in character with his teaching regarding the source of illness. We can see Jesus' point of view through various comments that he made while healing people. He said:

1. Illness can be a result of sin.

Later Jesus found him [a man he healed] at the temple and said to him, "See, you are well again. Stop sinning or something worse may happen to you."

—JOHN 5:14

2. Illness can occur without a fault.

As he [Jesus] went along, he saw a man blind from birth. His disciples asked him, "Rabbi, who sinned, this man or his parents, that he was born blind?" "Neither this man nor his parents sinned," said Jesus, "but this happened so that the work of God might be displayed in his life.

—JOHN 9:1–3

3. Illness can be caused by demons.

Then they brought him a demon-possessed man who was blind and mute, and Jesus healed him, so that he could both talk and see.

—MATTHEW 12:22;
SEE ALSO MATTHEW 9:32–34; MARK 7:31–37

Now that we've looked at physical healing, let's look at a spiritual type of healing—casting out demons.

CASTING OUT DEMONS

Both Muhammad and Jesus spoke about demons in their teachings. The issue I want to address here is what each one did about people who came to them for help against demons.

Muhammad

Muhammad, on the other hand, was not known for casting out demons. In fact, the Quran says that jinn (or demons) came to listen to Muhammad recite the Quran:

> Say (O Muhammad): "It has been revealed to me that a group of (from three to ten in number) jinn listened (to this Quran). They said: 'Verily, we have heard a wonderful Recitation' (this Quran)!
> —SURAH 72:1

This surah goes on to say that some of the jinn accepted Islam and became Muslims (Surah 72:14). When Muhammad prayed, they crowded around him to listen (Surah 72:19).

So Muhammad's relationship with demons was much different than Jesus'!

However, we do have an example of a woman coming to Muhammad and asking for help because she felt that she was being attacked by demons.

> A Muslim woman came to him and told him, "These unclean ones—demons—possess me and torment me and torture me." Muhammad said, "If you are patient in what you are walking through, you will come in Resurrection Day before Allah clean from any sin, and there will be no judgment against you. She said, "I swear in the name of the one who sent you that I will have patience until I meet Allah, but I am afraid that this demon will come and make me take my

clothes off (in public)"[that I will be sinning]. Then
Muhammad told her, "Every time you feel the demon
on you, you must go to Al-Ka'ba and wrap yourself in
the fabric that is draped over the Black Stone." Then
Muhammad prayed for her.[6]

Let's think about what Muhammad offered this woman. He
did not remove the demon from her. Instead he told her to endure
its harassment and said that she might get relief from going to the
Black Stone at Al-Ka'ba.

Muhammad's advice to her actually contradicts teaching in the
Quran, which says:

> And if an evil whisper comes to you from *Shaitan*
> (Satan), then seek refuge with Allah. Verily, He is All-
> Hearer, All-Knower.
>
> —SURAH 7:200

We can conclude easily that Muhammad did not present himself as being able to cast out demons.

Jesus

When Jesus encountered a person who was troubled by demons,
he told the demons to leave the person's body. A good example is
the story of the two crazed men Jesus encountered as they wan-
dered around the tombs in the region of Gadara. They were so
violent that people were afraid to travel that way. The demons in
these men begged Jesus, "If you drive us out, send us into the herd
of pigs." Jesus said to them, "Go!" and the demons came out of
the men (Matt. 8:28–34).

Other examples of Jesus casting out demons include:

- The man in the synagogue (Mark 1:23–28; Luke 4:
  33–37)

- A blind and mute man (Matt. 12:22)

- A mute man (Matt. 9:32–34)

- The daughter of a Canaanite woman (Matt. 15:21–28; Mark 7:24–30)

- A boy who suffered from convulsions (Matt. 17:14–21; Mark 9:14–30; Luke 9:37–43)

In addition to these specific stories, the Gospels often mention in general that Jesus cast out demons when the people came to him for help (Matt. 4:24; 8:16; Mark 1:34, 39). Jesus said he cast out demons by the power of God (Luke 11:14–28).

Now let us look at one area where the picture for Muhammad is hotly debated—miracles.

MIRACLES

Muhammad

We have already learned that Muhammad was not known for praying for physical healing or for casting out demons. Was he known for doing miracles?

As I mentioned at the beginning of this chapter, this is an area of debate among Muslims. Muslims look to the Quran as the greatest miracle. Aside from that, miracles do not play a major role in the story line of Muhammad. In other words, miracles were not described as drawing crowds to Muhammad. They did not have a big effect on how people treated him or how he spread his message.

With this background, let's look at the references to possible miracles by Muhammad.

A well-known story is the "splitting of the moon," described in hadith as follows:

> The people of Mecca asked the Prophet to show them a sign (miracle). So he showed them (the miracle) of the cleaving of the moon.[7]

The Quran makes reference to this in Surah 54:1:

> The Hour has drawn near, and the moon has been
> cleft asunder.

Many Muslims believe the moon literally split in half and appeared as two pieces in the sky. The date is thought to be in Mecca about five years before *hijra*. However, no reference is made to this miracle when Muhammad is challenged to deliver a sign. This is an unsolved problem.

All the other examples of miracles appear only in hadith and are not mentioned in the Quran. These include:

- Multiplying dates to repay a debt[8]

- Multiplying water
  - from a drinking utensil[9]
  - and from a well[10]
  - and from two bags of water borrowed from a woman on a camel[11]

- Producing rain after a drought in Medina[12]

- Lights leading two of Muhammad's companions through darkness[13]

- A date palm tree crying after Muhammad leaves[14]

- The ground spitting out the corpse of Christian who lied[15]

- A wolf speaking and inviting a man to follow Islam[16]

- Muhammad's Night Journey in which he reported being flown from Mecca to Jerusalem and seeing paradise and hell[17]

Jesus

Just as Jesus was popular because of his healings, he was also sought after because of miracles that he performed. A good example is when five thousand people came out to the desert to hear him teach, and they stayed so long that they became hungry. The disciples wanted to send them away, but when Jesus found five loaves of bread and two fish, he instructed the disciples to serve the people a meal. The miracle is that this small amount of bread and fish fed all the people. Later Jesus was hounded by people who remembered him multiplying the food (John 6:1–27).

Other examples of Jesus' miracles include:

- Turning water into wine at a wedding (John 2:1–11)

- Large catches of fish (Luke 5:1–11; John 21:1–14)

- Calming the storm as he and the disciples crossed a lake (Matt. 8:23–27; Mark 4:35–41; Luke 8:22–25)

- Feeding crowds with small amounts of food (Matt. 14:13–21; 15:32–38; Mark 6:34–44; 8:1–9; Luke 9: 12–17; John 6:1–15)

- Walking on water during a storm (Matt. 14:22–33; Mark 6:45–52; John 6:16–21)

- Finding money for taxes in the mouth of a fish (Matt. 17:24–28)

- Causing a fig tree to wither (Matt. 21:18–22; Mark 11: 20–25)

Although some of the miracles were performed in the presence of crowds (the miracle at the wedding and the multiplication of food), the other ones were seen only by his closest followers.

So there are accounts of miracles by both Muhammad and Jesus. What was the purpose of these miracles?

Muhammad's purpose for miracles

Some say his miracles were a sign of Muhammad's prophethood, but the Quran declared that the revelations to Muhammad were the only sign that would be given. It is an issue of debate.

Jesus' purpose for miracles

Jesus used his miracles as a sign that he was God, particularly for his followers. For example, Jesus' first miracle was turning water to wine at a wedding. This was an effective demonstration of power to his new followers.

Jesus also performed miracles out of compassion, particularly when multiplying food for a crowd.

> Jesus called his disciples to him and said, "I have compassion for these people; they have already been with me three days and have nothing to eat. I do not want to send them away hungry, or they may collapse on the way."
>
> —Matthew 15:32

HEALINGS AND MIRACLES BY THE FOLLOWERS

The last section of this chapter will look at whether Jesus or Muhammad taught their followers to practice healings and miracles.

Muhammad

Muhammad did not teach his followers to pray for healing or miracles. There is no hadith where Muhammad said, "If one of your relatives or children are sick, pray and ask for healing from Allah." There is no record in Islamic history of any of Muhammad's companions doing healings or miracles. This was not their method of spreading the message of Islam. Instead, after Muhammad's death, they remained organized in a military fashion and continued to spread Islam through jihad.

Jesus

Jesus expected his followers to do the same healings and miracles that he did and more.

> I tell you the truth, anyone who has faith in me will do what I have been doing. He will do even greater things than these, because I am going to the Father.
>
> —John 14:12

When Jesus sent his disciples out to preach, he told them:

> Heal the sick, raise the dead, cleanse those who have
> leprosy, drive out demons. Freely you have received,
> freely give.
> —MATTHEW 10:8; SEE ALSO MARK 3:15; LUKE 10:9

The question is: Were the disciples able to heal and cast out
demons like Jesus did? The answer was *yes*.

> They went out and preached that people should repent.
> They drove out many demons and anointed many sick
> people with oil and healed them.
> —MARK 6:12–13

> The seventy-two returned with joy and said, "Lord,
> even the demons submit to us in your name.
> —LUKE 10:17

The New Testament account after Jesus' death and resurrection
describes his followers performing "many wonders and miraculous signs" (Acts 2:43; see also Romans 15:19). For example:

- Lame man healed (Acts 3:1–10; 14:8–10)
- Husband and wife struck dead for lying (Acts 5:1–11)
- Disciples rescued from prison by an angel (Acts 5:
  19–20)
- Evil spirits came out; crippled and paralyzed people
  healed (Acts 8:6–13)
- Paralytic healed (Acts 9:32–35)
- Woman raised from the dead (Acts 9:36–41)
- False prophet blinded (Acts 13:8–11)
- Young man raised from dead after fall (Acts 20:9–12)
- No harm from a poisonous snake bite (Acts 28:3–5)

The people were attracted to the disciples and their message
because of the miracles and healings, just as they were attracted
Jesus.

CONCLUSION

Healing and miracles help us to see more differences between Jesus and Muhammad. Jesus' public activity was propelled by healing, casting out demons, and performing miracles. After his death and resurrection, his followers also attracted the people to their message through healing, casting out demons, and miracles.

In contrast, Islamic history records only a few stories of miracles associated with Muhammad and almost no stories regarding healings or casting out demons.

Since healings were the way Jesus effectively spread his message, let us now turn to the most effective way Muhammad spread his message—through *jihad*, or holy war.

13

The Meaning of
Holy War

B ecause you have already read about the life stories of Jesus and Muhammad, you will have an easy time understanding what they taught about war and the use of the sword. This chapter is divided into three sections:

First we will look at what Muhammad taught about tolerance of other religions and why moderate Muslims believe that jihad is not a physical battle but a spiritual battle. Then I will explain the two verses in the Gospels where Jesus talked about "swords." Muslims point to these verses to say that Jesus taught his followers to fight jihad. We will interpret these verses using other Gospel accounts.

Second, we will look at whether Muhammad considered jihad a permanent or temporary responsibility for Muslims. In contrast, we will review how Jesus taught his disciples to respond to their enemies.

Third, we will compare the rewards Muhammad offered his followers for fighting jihad with the rewards Jesus offered his followers for choosing *not* to fight.

The conclusion will address a question that is often raised by Christians and Muslims alike: Islamic history is bloody, but Christians have blood on their hands as well. So what is the difference between the wars that have been fought by Muslims and the wars fought by Christians?

MUHAMMAD AND THE SWORD

Tolerance vs. jihad

There are verses in the Quran that clearly call for tolerance:

> Let there be no compulsion in religion: Truth stands
> out clear from Error: whoever rejects Evil and believes
> in Allah has grasped the most trustworthy hand-hold,
> that never breaks. And Allah hears and knows all
> things.
> —SURAH 2:256, ALI TRANSLATION

This verse says, "You can't force anybody to change their religion. The right way should be obvious." Muhammad reported it during the beginning of his time in Medina, before the Battle of Badr.

Here is another verse of tolerance:

> And argue not with the people of the Scripture (Jews
> and Christians), unless it be in (a way) that is better
> (with good words and in good manner, inviting them
> to Islamic Monotheism with His Verses).
> —SURAH 29:46

This surah is believed to have been revealed in Mecca when Muslims were being harassed and persecuted. The verse says that Muslims should not argue with Jews and Christians; instead they should invite them to follow Islam. At this point, Muhammad still believed that most Jews and Christians would embrace Islam because of its belief in one God only.

However, in the same Quran you will find verses that clearly refer to fighting nonbelievers in the sense of a literal and physical fight where people are killed or taken prisoner. How do you reconcile these two conflicting commands? The key is to pay attention to when these verses were revealed. For example:

> Fight them until there is no more *Fitnah* (disbelief
> and polytheism, i.e. worshipping others besides

Allah) and the religion (worship) will be for Allah
Alone [in the whole of the world].

—SURAH 8:39

O Prophet (Muhammad)! Urge the believers to fight.
If there are twenty steadfast persons amongst you, they
will overcome two hundred, and if there be a hundred
steadfast persons they will overcome a thousand of
those who disbelieve, because they (the disbelievers)
are people who do not understand.

—SURAH 8:65

These verses were revealed in Medina *after* the Battle of Badr
(A.H. 2), the Muslims' surprising first victory against the army of
Mecca. Surah 2:256, the verse about tolerance, was revealed in
Medina *before* the Battle of Badr.

So which command is to be followed? In Muhammad's day the
answer was clear: The new cancelled out the old. People understood that when Muhammad said it was time to fight, this meant
that the time of tolerance was over. This principle is expressed in
the Quran in Surah 2:106:

Whatever a Verse (revelation) do We abrogate or cause
to be forgotten, We bring a better one or similar to it.
Know you not that Allah is able to do all things?

Muslim scholars refer to this as the principle of *naskh*. The idea
is that Muhammad's revelations were progressive. A new revelation canceled out an older revelation. This principle is not only
applied to jihad but also to many other issues as well including
drinking alcohol, validity of adoption, and the direction a person
faces for prayer.

Muhammad did not see these changes as contradictions.
He saw them as a *development* of the revelations. The Quran
explains:

And when We change a Verse (of the Quran,) in
place of another—and Allah knows best what He

sends down—they (the disbelievers) say: "You (O Muhammad) are but a *Muftari!* (forger, liar)." Nay, but most of them know not.

—SURAH 16:101

Is jihad a spiritual struggle?

Modern-day, moderate Muslims often say that jihad is a spiritual struggle within oneself to follow the teachings of Islam. Where do they get this idea? Some Muslims point to a story recorded in the hadith:

> Muhammad was returning from a battle when he told one of his friends, "We are returning from the little jihad to the great jihad."
>
> His friend asked him, "O prophet of Allah, what do you mean by the small battle and the great battle?"
>
> Muhammad replied, "The small battle is the battle we just came from where we were fighting the enemies of Islam. The great battle is the spiritual struggle of the Muslim life."[1]

In other words, on the way back home from a physical battle, it is reported that Muhammad said that the "greater jihad" was the spiritual battle within. This phrase "greater jihad" is used often by liberal Muslims.

There are some challenges to this hadith that you should know about.

1. Most importantly, it is inconsistent with the other teachings of Muhammad and the Quran. The Quran gives Muslims many guidelines for living, but the Quran never describes the struggle to follow these guidelines as "jihad."

2. The documentation that links this story to the actual life of Muhammad is weak. Orthodox Muslim scholars believe that Muhammad never said this.

Sheikh al-Elbeni, the most-respected scholar of hadith in the world, lists this as a weak hadith, even though it comes from otherwise reliable historians.

Even if the hadith is reliable, what does it really say? Does it cancel out the call for Muslims to fight the physical battles? Not explicitly. Did it explain to Muslims when their physical battle would be finished? No. Let's see if Muhammad ever gave an ending point for jihad.

The end of physical jihad

Let's look again at the Quran and see if it ever tells Muslims when to stop fighting holy war against unbelievers.

Nine years after emigrating to Medina (and less than two years before his death), Muhammad announced an important revelation regarding the Islamic attitude toward unbelievers. Muhammad made arrangements for these instructions to be read to the Muslims who had gone to Mecca for a pilgrimage.[2]

> Kill the *Mushrikun* [pagans] wherever you find them, and capture them and besiege them, and lie in wait for them in each and every ambush.
>
> —SURAH 9:5

> Fight against those who (1) believe not in Allah, (2) nor in the Last Day, (3) nor forbid that which has been forbidden by Allah and His Messenger (Muhammad) (4) and those who acknowledge not the religion of truth (i.e. Islam) among the people of the Scripture (Jews and Christians), until they pay the *Jizyah* [tax] with willing submission, and feel themselves subdued.
>
> —SURAH 9:29

As you can see, Muhammad continued to call for literal, physical jihad that ended only with the unbelievers being subdued.

The hadith also contain this exhortation from Muhammad:

> I heard the apostle of Allah say, I command by Allah
> to fight all the people till they say there is no god but
> Allah and I am his apostle. And whoever says that will
> save himself and his money.[3]

The Muslims took action on Muhammad's words. They took jihad to all peoples, attacking many countries in Asia, Africa, and Europe.

So it is hard to say that Muhammad gave an end point for jihad. However, modern Muslims have developed the idea that Muhammad only fought justified battles. Let's look at this point of view.

Justified war

While speaking across the United States, I often hear a familiar challenge: "Muhammad had to fight because he was defending his revelation and his people. His battles were justified."

Let's look at the verse from which people derived the term "just war," or "justified war."

> And do not kill anyone whose killing Allah has
> forbidden, except for a just cause. And whoever is
> killed wrongfully...We have given his heir the authority
> [to demand *Qisas*—Law of Equality in punishment—or
> to forgive, or to take *Diyah* (blood money)].
> —SURAH 17:33

This verse is not talking about war. It refers to a murder that is committed in society. The verse ends by describing the rights of the victim's family. It is part of a passage in the Quran that gives guidelines for daily life, such as honoring parents, giving to the poor, sexual morality, and the treatment of orphans, among other things. This verse, however, provides a source for the term "just war."

Now let's look at other verses that speak more directly to the issue of war.

They say Muhammad only sanctioned war when there was a just

cause, in other words, when Muslims were persecuted or attacked first. Here are some of the verses used to support this idea:

> To those against whom war is made, permission is given (to fight), because they are wronged.
> —SURAH 22:39, ALI TRANSLATION

> Fight in the cause of Allah those who fight you, but do not transgress limits, for Allah does not love transgressors. And slay them wherever you catch them, and turn them out from where they turned you out....Fight them on until there is no more tumult or oppression and there prevail justice and faith in Allah; but if they cease, let there be no hostility except to those who practice oppression.
> —SURAH 2:190–193, ALI TRANSLATION

> "If they incline to peace, you also incline to it, and (put your) trust in Allah. Verily, He is the All-Hearer, the All-Knower."
> —SURAH 8:61

Did Muhammad practice justified war—only attacking when he had been attacked first (having a "just cause")? This could be considered somewhat true for his attacks against Mecca because the Meccans had given Muhammad and his people trouble when Muhammad lived among them. However, the Meccans did not follow Muhammad to Medina and attack him there. They left him alone. Muhammad was the one who struck first, attacking a caravan returning to Mecca from Syria.

Some say Muhammad's attacks against the Jewish communities were justified because the Jews tried to work with the Meccans to attack Muhammad during the Battle of the Trench. However, the Jews and Meccans were completely unsuccessful during the battle, and they did not harm Muhammad at all. The Jews were not a serious threat to Islam.

But after Muhammad had conquered all those people who were a threat to Islam, he continued to expand jihad to those who posed no threat to him. He began sending letters out to kings and rulers outside of Arabia, calling for them to submit to Islam.

After his death, his followers also continued to introduce jihad into countries that had not been aggressive toward the Islamic state. For example, Egypt never attacked Muslims, but the Islamic army came and killed more than four million Egyptians during the first century of Islam.

Muslims did not stop after Egypt: they went south to Sudan and west to conquer all of North Africa. What did the countries of North Africa do to provoke Muhammad or his successors? Nothing.

What danger was Spain, Portugal, and Southern Europe to Islam and Muhammad's successors? Islam attacked them, too.

My conclusion is that neither Muhammad nor his followers restricted themselves to "justified wars." The only way to avoid the sword of Islam was to submit.

Now let's look at what Jesus said about war.

JESUS AND THE SWORD

Why do Muslims think Jesus called for jihad?

Many Muslims believe that Jesus himself called for holy war. They point to Matthew 10:34–35 where Jesus was giving his twelve disciples instructions about going out to preach on their own.

> Do not suppose that I have come to bring peace to the earth. I did not come to bring peace, but a sword. For I have come to turn "a man against his father, a daughter against her mother, a daughter-in-law against her mother-in-law—a man's enemies will be the members of his own household."

Muslims say, "Look—Jesus said that he came to bring a sword to earth." However, Jesus' intended meaning for this passage becomes clear by looking at the same teaching as recorded in a different Gospel. Luke reported that Jesus said:

> Do you think I came to bring peace on earth? No,
> I tell you, but division. From now on there will be
> five in one family divided against each other, three
> against two and two against three.
>
> —LUKE 12:51–52

Jesus was warning his disciples that his message would be divisive. Rather than bringing people together, it would tear people apart—even family members would become enemies. Jesus explained that some converts would die at the hands of their brothers, fathers, or children:

> Brother will betray brother to death, and a father his
> child; children will rebel against their parents and have
> them put to death.
>
> —MATTHEW 10:21

In other words, Jesus declared that his message would cause people to bring out their swords to attack those who chose to follow him.

As a Christian convert from a Muslim country, I can tell you that Jesus' warning applies today. To my great sorrow, when I told my father I had chosen to follow Jesus, he tried to shoot me with his handgun. However, I have experienced only a little trouble compared to the fate of some Muslims who choose Christianity.

If we look at other parts of Jesus' message to his disciples that day, we see more evidence that the sword would not be in the hands of the believers, but on their necks. Rather than wielding the sword, they would be the victims of it.

> Be on your guard against men; they will hand you over
> to the local councils and flog you in their synagogues.
>
> —MATTHEW 10:17

> Do not be afraid of those who kill the body but cannot
> kill the soul.
>
> —MATTHEW 10:28

> Whoever loses his life for my sake will find it.
> —MATTHEW 10:39

Jesus told his disciples to buy swords.

Some Muslims will also point to another saying of Jesus about swords. This one occurred after Jesus ate his final meal with his disciples before he was arrested and put to death. Jesus reminded them of their previous preaching journeys.

> Then Jesus asked them, "When I sent you without purse, bag or sandals, did you lack anything?"
> "Nothing," they answered.
> —LUKE 22:35

Then Jesus gave them new instructions:

> "But now if you have a purse, take it, and also a bag; and if you don't have a sword, sell your cloak and buy one...."
> The disciples said, "See, Lord, here are two swords."
> "That is enough," he replied.
> —LUKE 22:36, 38

The word *sword* in this verse refers to a dagger or short sword that travelers used for protection against robbers or wild animals.

Luke does not record any more explanation of these instructions. However, later that same night, Peter used one of the disciples' two swords. Let's see how Jesus responded.

Jesus went out as usual to the Mount of Olives to pray, and his disciples went with him. A large crowd armed with swords and clubs confronted them. As the people came toward Jesus to arrest him, Peter drew out one of the swords and struck at the servant of the high priest, cutting off his ear. Jesus said to Peter:

> Put your sword back in its place...for all who draw the sword will die by the sword. Do you think I cannot call on my Father, and he will at once put at my disposal more than twelve legions of angels? But then

> how would the Scriptures be fulfilled that say it must
> happen this way?
>
> —MATTHEW 26:52–54

After Jesus rebuked Peter, he healed the servant's ear, and Peter put his sword away. The armed group took Jesus before the high priest, who would eventually have him crucified. So when we look at the events on the night of Jesus' arrest, we can see that Jesus did not intend for the disciples to use their swords to defend him.

But what was Jesus' intention? Here is my understanding. Jesus wanted his disciples to know that after his death, they would not be as safe as before. During their travels, they would need to carry money to buy food and swords to protect themselves.

Is there any possibility that Jesus was asking them to organize a militia in order to protect or promote his teachings? No. This would be too inconsistent with the teaching of Jesus' entire life. As further evidence, after Jesus' death, there is no evidence that the disciples began to gather weapons. In fact, the only sword mentioned in the biblical record of the early church belonged to a jailer who was guarding Paul and Silas (Acts 16:27).

JESUS' RESPONSE TO HIS ENEMIES

Jesus walked away from threats.

In his own life, when Jesus was threatened, he did not fight back. He walked away.

> After this, Jesus went around in Galilee, purposely staying away from Judea because the Jews there were waiting to take his life.
>
> —JOHN 7:1

> But the Pharisees went out and plotted how they might kill Jesus. Aware of this, Jesus withdrew from that place.
>
> — MATTHEW 12:14–15

> All the people in the synagogue were furious when they heard this. They got up, drove him out of the town, and

took him to the brow of the hill on which the town was built, in order to throw him down the cliff. But he walked right through the crowd and went on his way.

—LUKE 4:28–30

At this, they picked up stones to stone him, but Jesus hid himself, slipping away from the temple grounds.

—JOHN 8:59

This is the same response Jesus instructed his twelve disciples to make when they were threatened:

When you are persecuted in one place, flee to another.

—MATTHEW 10:23

If anyone will not welcome you or listen to your words, shake the dust off your feet when you leave that home or town.

—MATTHEW 10:14

This is what his followers practiced as recorded in the Acts of the Apostles.

[After Stephen was martyred] a great persecution broke out against the church at Jerusalem, and all except the apostles were scattered throughout Judea and Samaria....Those who had been scattered preached the word wherever they went.

—ACTS 8:1, 4

So Saul stayed with them and moved about freely in Jerusalem, speaking boldly in the name of the Lord. He talked and debated with the Grecian Jews, but they tried to kill him. When the brothers learned of this, they took him down to Caesarea and sent him off to Tarsus.

—ACTS 9:28–30

But the Jews incited the God-fearing women of high standing and the leading men of the city. They stirred up persecution against Paul and Barnabas, and expelled them from their region. So they shook the dust from

their feet in protest against them and went to Iconium.
[Jesus had instructed the disciples to "shake the dust
off their feet" when rejected.]

—ACTS 13:50–51

There was a plot afoot among the Gentiles and Jews,
together with their leaders, to mistreat them and
stone them. But they found out about it and fled to
the Lycaonian cities of Lystra and Derbe and to the
surrounding country, where they continued to preach
the good news.

—ACTS 14:5–7

Jesus refused to punish people for rejecting him.

As the time of his death was nearing, Jesus set out for Jerusalem
with his disciples. As they approached a village of the Samaritans,
Jesus sent some messengers ahead of the group to make preparations for their arrival. But the Samaritans rejected the messengers
because they were very bitter about the way they were treated by
the Jews.

When the disciples James and John saw this, they asked, "Lord,
do you want us to call fire down from heaven to destroy them?"

If Jesus had said, "This is a powerful idea, My disciple. I will
ask My father to send a fire to destroy this village," then we will
have the evidence to say that Jesus told his disciples to use holy war
against others. However, look at what Jesus did:

But Jesus turned and rebuked them, and they went to
another village.

—LUKE 9:55–56

Jesus refused to fight for freedom from Rome.

In Jesus' day, the Jews hated living under the authority of Rome,
and many of them were looking for a Messiah who would overthrow Rome and establish an earthly kingdom. However, Jesus
submitted to Roman authority:

> Then the Pharisees went out and laid plans to trap him
> in his words.…"Tell us then, what is your opinion?
> Is it right to pay taxes to Caesar or not?" But Jesus,
> knowing their evil intent, said, "You hypocrites, why
> are you trying to trap me? Show me the coin used for
> paying the tax." They brought him a denarius, and
> he asked them, "Whose portrait is this? And whose
> inscription?" "Caesar's," they replied. Then he said to
> them, "Give to Caesar what is Caesar's, and to God
> what is God's."
>
> —MATTHEW 22:15, 17–21

He refused to allow people to set him up as an earthly king.
After Jesus had fed five thousand people with five loaves and two
fish, the people began to say:

> "Surely this is the Prophet who is to come into the
> world." Jesus, knowing that they intended to come and
> make him king by force, withdrew again to a mountain
> by himself.
>
> —JOHN 6:14–15

While Jesus refused to establish a political kingdom on earth,
Muhammad made great effort to establish a physical kingdom for
Islam on earth. He reported that Allah would be very pleased with
those who helped him, especially those who fought on the battlefield for Allah's cause.

ISLAM'S REWARDS FOR HOLY WAR

Muhammad described many rewards for those who fought—
both in the present world and in the life after death.

> Whatever you shall spend in the Cause of Allah shall
> be repaid unto you, and you shall not be treated
> unjustly.
>
> —SURAH 8:60

Rewards in the present world include:

Wealth

Muhammad reserved a fifth of the spoils of war and divided the rest among his military. The Quran makes several references to booty and the spoils of war. For example:

> So enjoy what you have gotten of booty in war, lawful and good, and be afraid of Allah. Certainly, Allah is Oft-Forgiving, Most Merciful.
>
> —SURAH 8:69

> Allah has promised you abundant spoils that you will capture, and He has hastened for you this, and He has restrained the hands of men from you, that it may be a sign for the believers, and that He may guide you to a Straight Path.
>
> —SURAH 48:20

Allah's love

> Verily, Allah loves those who fight in His Cause in rows (ranks) as if they were a solid structure.
>
> —SURAH 61:4

> Allah has preferred in grades those who strive hard and fight with their wealth and their lives above those who sit (at home). Unto each, Allah has promised good (Paradise), but Allah has preferred those who strive hard and fight, above those who sit (at home) by a huge reward.
>
> —SURAH 4:95

Sins forgiven

> [If] you strive hard and fight in the Cause of Allah with your wealth and your lives...He will forgive you your sins, and admit you into Gardens under which rivers flow.
>
> —SURAH 61:11–12

Avoiding Allah's anger

Allah does not love those who refuse to fight.

> If any do turn his back to them on such a day—unless it be in a stratagem of war, or to retreat to a troop (of his own)—he draws on himself the wrath of Allah, and his abode is Hell—an evil refuge (indeed)!
>
> —SURAH 8:16, ALI TRANSLATION

Rewards in the afterlife include:

Paradise

Muhammad encouraged people to go to battle in order to earn paradise.

> While facing the enemy...the Messenger of Allah said: Surely, the gates of Paradise are under the shadows of the swords. A man in a shabby condition got up and said; Abu Musa, did you hear the Messenger of Allah say this? He said: Yes. (The narrator said): He returned to his friends and said: I greet you (a farewell greeting). Then he broke the sheath of his sword, threw it away, advanced with his (naked) sword towards the enemy and fought (them) with it until he was slain.[4]

Virgins

Muhammad said the gardens of paradise would provide men with beautiful virgins to use for their pleasure.

> In them will be (Maidens) chaste, restraining their glances, whom no man or Jinn before them has touched.
>
> —SURAH 55:56, ALI TRANSLATION

> In them [the Gardens] will be fair (Companions), good, beautiful.
>
> —SURAH 55:70, ALI TRANSLATION

JESUS' REWARDS FOR PEACE, MERCY, AND FORGIVENESS

Jesus never talked about fighting in the name of God, so of course he didn't promise any rewards for doing so. However, Jesus did speak of rewards for those who refused to fight.

This teaching is summed up in Jesus' famous Sermon on the Mount. He began by listing the type of people who are "blessed." Some of these include:

> Blessed are the merciful,
>   for they will be shown mercy....
> Blessed are the peacemakers,
>   for they will be called sons of God.
> Blessed are those who are persecuted because of
>   righteousness,
>   for theirs is the kingdom of heaven.
>
> Blessed are you when people insult you, persecute you
> and falsely say all kinds of evil against you because of me.
>   —MATTHEW 5:7, 9–11

Then he explained God's requirement for entering the kingdom of heaven: it was righteousness that exceeded the righteousness of law. It was a righteousness that went beyond outside actions and, instead, went deeper to the attitude of the heart.

In his sermon, Jesus applied this concept to many subjects, but let's look at what he said related to war and revenge.

> You have heard that it was said, "Eye for eye, and tooth for tooth." But I tell you, Do not resist an evil person. If someone strikes you on the right cheek, turn to him the other also. And if someone wants to sue you and take your tunic, let him have your cloak as well. If someone forces you to go one mile, go with him two miles. Give to the one who asks you, and do not turn away from the one who wants to borrow from you.
>
> You have heard that it was said, "Love your neighbor

and hate your enemy." But I tell you: Love your enemies
and pray for those who persecute you, that you may
be sons of your Father in heaven. He causes his sun
to rise on the evil and the good, and sends rain on the
righteous and the unrighteous. If you love those who
love you, what reward will you get?

—MATTHEW 5:38–46

So in everything, do to others what you would have them
do to you, for this sums up the Law and the Prophets.

—MATTHEW 7:12

WHAT ABOUT THE CRUSADES?

In this chapter we've looked at an important area where Jesus
and Muhammad were very different. In the same way that Jesus
was known for healings and miracles, Muhammad was known
for fighting jihad. However, there is one question about war
that we have not addressed.

Whether I am speaking with Muslims or Christians, if we go
to the topic of holy war, I am always confronted by the question:
What about the Crusades? People want to point out that even
though Islam has a bloody history, Christianity does as well. Here
is how I answered that question a few years ago during a debate
with the president of the department of Islamic study at Rau
University in Johannesburg, South Africa. About two hundred
students were in the audience.

When this professor asked me why I left Islam, I told him,
"I studied the history of Islam in a very deep way, and it is
simply an ocean of blood. When Muslims stopped killing non-
Muslims, they turned and started to kill each other." Then
I gave him examples: the War of Conversion that claimed the
lives of almost ninety thousand people who tried to stop paying
the *zakat*, or charity tax, after Muhammad's death; the War of
Sufyan, where ten thousand Muslims died fighting over who
would be in charge of the Islamic state after Muhammad's
death; the Iran/Iraq War, in which one million people were

killed and two million disabled in the course of nine years; civil war in Algeria, where 150,000 people have been killed in the past seven years.

He responded: "Christians also use holy war. They are fulfilling biblical teachings to use the sword. Jesus said in Matthew 10:34: 'I came not to bring peace but a sword.'" He reminded me: "Look at the Crusades. Look at Ireland. Look at Yugoslavia and what Serbian Christians did to the Muslims."

I didn't address the real meaning of Matthew 10:34 at that time, but I told him, "Fine. This happened and will continue to happen both in Islam and Christianity. But the fact is that when Muslims used the sword, they practiced the Quranic teaching of holy war presented by many verses and chapters and put in action by the very founder of Islam. But I challenge you to find any Scripture where Jesus commanded his disciples to go and to kill in the name of Jesus Christ.

"And what you told me about the evils done by Christians—these people were Christians by name only. They disobeyed the word of Christ and they were led astray by the desires of their hearts. The Bible says, 'The heart of man is deceitful.' Because of this, you will see no difference between the actions of Muslims who kill and destroy and the actions of Christians who kill and destroy. The difference is in whether or not they are following the example of their leader."

The professor had no more to say after this answer. He just moved on to another topic.

The simple fact is that every person who participated in the Crusades was going against the teachings of Jesus. These people could carry crosses, but they were not following Christ. However, when Muslims overthrow a government by force, they are following both the teachings and example of Muhammad.

AN INTERESTING COMPARISON

There are two interesting anecdotes about Jesus and Muhammad that sum up their differences about holy war.

> One day after battle, Muhammad came back to his home and called his daughter Fatima. He said, "Wash the blood from this sword and I swear in the name of Allah this sword was obeying me all the time." He then took the swords of his friend Ali ibn Abu Talib and washed them for him.[5]

So Muhammad asked his daughter to wash his sword, which he would have normally done by himself, and then he in turn honored his cousin Ali by washing his sword.

Let's see how Jesus honored his followers.

> So he got up from the meal, took off his outer clothing, and wrapped a towel around his waist. After that, he poured water into a basin and began to wash his disciples' feet, drying them with the towel that was wrapped around him.
>
> When he had finished washing their feet, he put on his clothes and returned to his place. "Do you understand what I have done for you?" he asked them. "You call me 'Teacher' and 'Lord,' and rightly so, for that is what I am. Now that I, your Lord and Teacher, have washed your feet, you also should wash one another's feet. I have set you an example that you should do as I have done for you. I tell you the truth, no servant is greater than his master, nor is a messenger greater than the one who sent him. Now that you know these things, you will be blessed if you do them.
>
> —JOHN 13:4–5, 12–17

Muhammad washed his follower's swords; Jesus washed his follower's feet. There is no simpler way to sum up their differences.

DIFFERENCES AND SIMILARITIES

The more you know about Jesus and Muhammad, the more you see their fundamental differences. Yet many westerners keep looking for similarities. Some writers work hard to find verses from the Bible and verses from the Quran that sound similar and put them side by side.[6] Their goal is to reduce animosity between Muslims, Jews, and Christians and to bring people together. This is a noble goal.

However, in searching for matching passages, it is easy to lose sight of the big picture. In the next chapter we will look at a topic that is easily distorted—love. Rather than compare isolated verses, we will look at the overall picture presented by Jesus and Muhammad—and discover more significant differences.

14

Teachings About Love

When I was living as a Muslim in Egypt, I was always puzzled by a little saying that the Christians used to put on their cars or frame in their shops. The phrase was *Allah Mahabe*, or *God is love*. These two words are never put together in the Quran. I always thought, *I wonder what these people are trying to say.*

In this chapter my goal is to present a good characterization about what Jesus and Muhammad taught regarding love.

Love must always be understood in the context of a relationship. So as we look at their teachings about love, we are going to discover the nature of the important relationships in Jesus and Muhammad's lives. These relationships revolve around four points:

- God
- His Messenger
- The Believers
- The Unbelievers

Please refer to the graphic on the opposite page. There are a few descriptive words to guide you; however, the purpose of the rest of this chapter is to explain these relationships. Special attention is given to looking for love between these different points.

Let's start by looking at the relationship that guides all the others—the relationship between God and his messenger.

Jesus and Muhammad:
Their Key Relationships

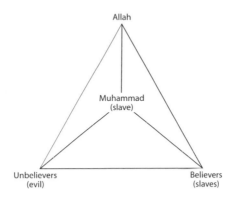

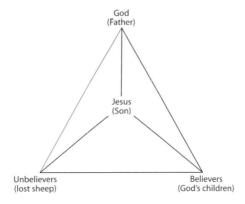

THE RELATIONSHIP BETWEEN GOD
AND HIS MESSENGER

Muhammad

Muhammad described himself as a slave of Allah. (See Surah 2:23.) The Quran or the hadith do not talk about Muhammad loving Allah or about Allah loving Muhammad. Muhammad's position was one of a slave empowered by his master's authority.

He who obeys the Messenger (Muhammad), has indeed obeyed Allah.

—SURAH 4:80

And whatsoever the Messenger (Muhammad) gives you, take it; and whatsoever he forbids you, abstain (from it).

—SURAH 59:7

And whoever contradicts and opposes the Messenger (Muhammad) after the right path has been shown clearly to him, and follows other than the believers' way, We shall keep him in the path he has chosen, and burn him in Hell—what an evil destination!

—SURAH 4:115

Jesus

Jesus described his relationship with God as a son to a father. This was a relationship of mutual love.

When Jesus was being baptized, the Gospel writers report that a voice from heaven said, "This is my Son, whom I love; with him I am well pleased" (Matt. 17:5; see also Matt. 12:18).

Jesus spoke of obeying and loving God, but not of fearing him.

I love the Father and...I do exactly what my Father has commanded me.

—JOHN 14:31

Jesus turned to God the Father for comfort. The night before his crucifixion he prayed,

Abba, Father, everything is possible for you. Take this cup from me. Yet not what I will, but what you will.

—MARK 14:36

As he turned to God for comfort, Jesus called him "Abba," the Aramaic word a child would use when speaking to a parent. It was like saying "Daddy." So we see a picture of a personal, loving relationship between Jesus and God.

THE RELATIONSHIP BETWEEN
THE MESSENGER AND PEOPLE

Muhammad

Just as Muhammad called himself a slave to Allah, he said that other Muslims were slaves as well (Surah 50:8).

The Quran puts little emphasis on loving Allah, although it does occasionally mention love for him (Surah 2:165). Instead, it calls for obedience to Allah. What happens if a slave does not obey? He is punished.

> And whoever defies and disobeys Allah and His Messenger, then verily, Allah is Severe in punishment.
> —SURAH 8:13

The revelations said those who disobeyed should be punished, and Muhammad carried out the sentence. For example, the revelations forbid Muslims to drink alcohol. Therefore, Muhammad punished those who disobeyed this law.

> Abu Huraira said, "A man who drank wine was brought to the Prophet. The Prophet said, 'Beat him!'" Abu Huraira added, "So some of us beat him with our hands, and some with their shoes, and some with their garments (by twisting it) like a lash."[1]

The punishment for stealing was to have your right hand cut off. A group of people asked Muhammad to make an exception for a certain woman who had been caught stealing. This is how Muhammad responded.

> Usama approached the Prophet on behalf of a woman (who had committed theft). The Prophet said, "The people before you were destroyed because they used to inflict the legal punishments on the poor and forgive the rich. By Him in Whose Hand my soul is! If Fatima (the daughter of the Prophet) did that (i.e. stole), I would cut off her hand."[2]

If you ask a Muslim, Do you know how much Allah loves you? he will respond, "I don't know how much he loves me. Only Allah knows." Muslims must wait until Judgment Day to find out if Allah loves them and will invite them into paradise.

We see that Allah has a stern relationship with believers. What does Allah think of unbelievers?

> Verily Allah guides not those whom He makes to go astray....And they will have no helpers.
>
> —SURAH 16:37

Allah purposes for some people to be led astray in order to populate the hell he created.

> If We had so willed, We could certainly have brought every soul its true guidance: but the Word from Me will come true, "I will fill Hell with Jinns and men all together."
>
> —SURAH 32:13, ALI TRANSLATION

Allah does not love unbelievers.

Jesus

The love relationship between Jesus and God the Father was reflected in Jesus' relationship with his followers. Jesus told his disciples that God loved them:

> The Father himself loves you because you have loved me and have believed that I came from God.
>
> —JOHN 16:27

Jesus also said that he loved his followers:

> As the Father loved me, so have I loved you.
>
> —JOHN 15:9

Jesus said that he cared for the believers just as a shepherd cares for his sheep.

> I am the good shepherd; I know my sheep and my sheep know me—just as the Father knows me and

I know the Father—and I lay down my life for the
sheep.

—JOHN 10:14–15

Jesus loved his followers, but did he love unbelievers? According
to his actions, the answer is *yes*.

- He ate with tax collectors and sinners (Luke 15:1–2).

- He shared his message personally with a Samaritan
  woman who was living with a man who was not her
  husband (John 4:1–26).

- He allowed a woman known to be a sinner to wash
  his feet while he was at a dinner with religious leaders
  (Luke 7:36–50).

- He accepted the repentance of the "criminal" who
  hung on the cross next to him during his crucifixion
  (Luke 23:39–43).

Jesus had the attitude that he was sent to help sinners.

> Jesus said to them, "It is not the healthy who need
> a doctor, but the sick. I have not come to call the
> righteous, but sinners."
>
> —MARK 2:17

Jesus said God sent him to the world because God loved the
world—those who had not yet believed on him. (See Romans 5:8.)

Jesus said the Most High is "kind to the ungrateful and wicked"
(Luke 6:35).

THE RELATIONSHIP BETWEEN
BELIEVERS AND UNBELIEVERS

So far we have looked at the primary relationship—God and his
messenger—and how that is played out in the relationship between
the messenger and his followers. We focused on evidence of love.

Now we turn to the instructions Muhammad and Jesus gave their followers about loving each other and loving unbelievers.

Muhammad

Similar to Jesus, Muhammad taught that Muslims must hold to a high standard in their behavior toward each other:

> And hold fast, all of you together, to the Rope of Allah (i.e., this Quran), and be not divided among yourselves, and remember Allah's Favour on you, for you were enemies one to another but He joined your hearts together, so that, by His Grace, you became brethren (in Islamic faith).
>
> —SURAH 3:103

> Muhammad is the messenger of Allah. And those who are with him are severe against disbelievers, and merciful among themselves.
>
> —SURAH 48:29

> The believers are nothing else than brothers (in Islamic religion). So make reconciliation between your brothers, and fear Allah, that you may receive mercy.
>
> —SURAH 49:10

Yet Muhammad called for Muslims to have a completely different attitude toward nonbelievers.

Before jihad was instituted, he warned Muslims to reject non-Muslims as friends:

> O you who believe! Take not My enemies and your enemies (i.e. disbelievers and polytheists) as friends, showing affection toward them, while they have disbelieved in what has come to you of the truth...and have driven out the Messenger and yourselves (from your homeland) because you believe in Allah your Lord!
>
> —SURAH 60:1

After jihad began, he called Muslims to participate in holy war against unbelievers, killing them if necessary in order to make them submit to Islam.

Jesus

In his final words with his disciples before his death, Jesus told them:

> A new command I give you: Love one another. As I have loved you, so you must love one another. By this all men will know that you are my disciples, if you love one another.
>
> —JOHN 13:34–35

Are Christians following this command very well? Sometimes I don't think so. But this is the standard that Jesus set. Jesus said that to inherit eternal life you must "love the Lord your God…and, 'Love your neighbor as yourself'" (Luke 10:27). A religious ruler wanted to justify his attitude toward people he didn't like so he asked Jesus, "Who is my neighbor?" Jesus replied:

> A man was going down from Jerusalem to Jericho, when he fell into the hands of robbers. They stripped him of his clothes, beat him and went away, leaving him half dead. A priest happened to be going down the same road, and when he saw the man, he passed by on the other side. So too, a Levite, when he came to the place and saw him, passed by on the other side. But a Samaritan, as he traveled, came where the man was; and when he saw him, he took pity on him. He went to him and bandaged his wounds, pouring on oil and wine. Then he put the man on his own donkey, took him to an inn and took care of him. The next day he took out two silver coins and gave them to the innkeeper. "Look after him," he said, "and when I return, I will reimburse you for any extra expense you may have."
>
> Which of these three do you think was a neighbor to the man who fell into the hands of robbers?

> The expert in the law replied, "The one who had
> mercy on him." Jesus told him, "Go and do likewise."
> —LUKE 10:30–37

Through this parable Jesus taught: your neighbor is not only someone from your own country or someone who shares your beliefs. Your neighbor can be anyone around you.

How else did Jesus ask his followers to love nonbelievers? He told them to go out and preach the good news to them, to heal their sick, to cast out demons, and to raise the dead.

CONCLUSION

The most important point of this chapter is that Jesus and Muhammad describe the nature of God in very different ways—for Jesus, God is a loving father; for Muhammad, Allah is a demanding master. This description sets the tone regarding love for all their other relationships. To bring this point home, let's imagine that a believer has left the faith. What did Muhammad say Allah would do? What did Jesus say God would do?

The Quran says:

> O you who believe! Whoever from among you turns
> back from his religion (Islam), Allah will bring a people
> whom He will love and they will love Him; humble
> towards the believers, stern towards the disbelievers,
> fighting in the Way of Allah, and never fear of the
> blame of the blamers. That is the Grace of Allah which
> He bestows on whom He wills.
> —SURAH 5:54

This verse explains that if a person leaves Islam, then Allah will bring other people that are better. Allah does not mourn for the ones who leave him or seek to bring them back. He gets better people.

Surah 39:7 also says: "If you reject (Allah), truly Allah has no need of you" (ALI TRANSLATION).

Now look at the story Jesus told about a shepherd who had one hundred sheep and lost one.

Suppose one of you has a hundred sheep and loses one of them. Does he not leave the ninety-nine in the open country and go after the lost sheep until he finds it? And when he finds it, he joyfully puts it on his shoulders and goes home. Then he calls his friends and neighbors together and says, "Rejoice with me; I have found my lost sheep." I tell you that in the same way there will be more rejoicing in heaven over one sinner who repents than over ninety-nine righteous persons who do not need to repent.

—LUKE 15:4–7; SEE ALSO VERSES 8–10

Allah finds new believers who will serve him better. In contrast, God the Father searches for the one lost lamb until he finds it and brings it home rejoicing. This is the difference between Allah and God.

Jesus and Muhammad described the nature of God very differently, but they both instructed their followers to pray. In the next chapter we will compare Jesus and Muhammad's teachings on prayer. You will see that their different beliefs about the nature of God greatly affected their approaches to prayer and their expectations about how God would respond.

15

Teachings on Prayer

It's amazing that one word—*prayer*—can have two meanings that are so different. Jesus and Muhammad both taught their followers to pray, but their method and purpose of prayer were totally different.

In this chapter I will describe for you the Muslim lifestyle of prayer that I lived for thirty years. If you are a Muslim, you will already understand exactly what I am talking about. However, if you have never practiced Islam, much of this information will be new to you. I've gone into extra detail for your sake. After establishing Muhammad's teachings on prayer, I will describe Jesus teaching his disciples how to pray and how that teaching impacted me the first time I read it.

THE PATTERN OF PRAYER

My family took me to the mosque from the time I was a toddler. When I reached the age of six or seven, I was require to go to the mosque to pray five times a day. Growing up in a devout family in Egypt, this was a part of our lifestyle. As a child, I have vivid memories of getting up for first prayers, around 3:30 a.m., on cold winter mornings. Prayer saturated my life.

After graduating from Al-Azhar high school when I was eighteen, I was qualified to lead the prayers. My uncle occasionally gave me the opportunity to lead prayers at his mosque.

After I earned my bachelor's degree from Al-Azhar, I spent a year in the Egyptian army and led the prayers at the mosque at our base.

After I finished my master's degree, I was given leadership of a small mosque and conducted first, fourth, and fifth prayers.

Every day of my life—from childhood through the time when I was imprisoned by the Egyptian police—I prayed five times a day. To put it simply, I've said a lot of Muslim prayers.

In Islam, the five daily prayers are a scripted event made up of both words and physical movement. Each unit of prayer is called a *raka'ah* [RA-kuh-ah]. Let me walk you through the pattern of one raka'ah.

THE WASHING

Imagine you have permission to be on the campus of Al-Azhar University as the call for the third prayer of the day goes out at about 3 p.m. If you were there, this is what you would experience.

Everywhere activity stops. Anyone who has become impure (by using the bathroom or touching a woman or dog, etc.) must cleanse himself before prayer. Whoever needs to perform the ceremonial washing goes to a bathroom in the academic building or goes to the large bathroom at the back of the university mosque.

Before he washes, he says these words: "I put my face to the true creator, and I begin my washing." Then he follows these steps.

1. He washes his hands. First he washes the right hand and then the left hand. Each hand is washed to the wrist only—three times.

2. He rinses his mouth with water. He uses his right finger to rub his teeth—three times.

3. He cleans his nose with water—three times.

4. He washes his face with water going from the hairline, around the ear, and under the chin—three times.

5. He washes his arms, from the wrist to the elbow, right hand first—three times.

6. He washes his hair by dipping his hand in water and smoothing it over his hair—one time.

7. He washes his ears with a wet finger. There is a specific direction and motion he must use to do this.

8. He washes his feet up to his ankles; the right foot first—three times each.

This is the washing all Muslims perform in order to stand before Allah. This is what Muhammad did, and he is the Muslims' example, so that is what Muslims do.

THE FIRST HALF OF A RAKA'AH

After washing, everyone goes inside the university mosque in the center of the campus, and they line up in straight rows facing Mecca (in Saudi Arabia). About eight hundred to one thousand people are in the mosque. The prayer leader cups his hands behind his ears and declares, "Allah is great." Everyone repeats back to him, "Allah is great."

Then all together they cross their hands over their stomachs, right hand on top, and recite the first chapter of the Quran in Arabic. No matter what language a Muslim speaks, this chapter must be quoted in Arabic.

For the next few seconds, the prayer leader allows time for each person to quote additional verses from the Quran. It is up to the individual as to how many verses he quotes during the time the prayer leader allows.

Then the leader cups his hands behind his ears and calls out again: "Allah is great."

In unison, they bow at the waist with their hands on their knees and respond, "I praise my great Lord."

This makes up the first half of the raka'ah. The second half of the raka'ah begins immediately.

THE SECOND HALF OF A RAKA'AH

First they kneel together by touching their knees to the ground first, then hands, and finally bowing with their foreheads touching the ground. Then they say, "I praise my Lord, the very high One" three times. They remain with their foreheads on the ground until the leader directs them to sit up. Then they sit up and lean back on their heels, with their legs crossed at the ankle and the left foot turned in. Muhammad crossed his ankles this way and, therefore, so do Muslims. This pattern is repeated three times.

During this cycle is their opportunity to make requests to Allah. Muhammad taught that when a man's forehead was on the ground, he was closest to Allah. This was his moment to pray for his family or others. When I had a lot of requests for Allah, I remember praying as fast as I could while my forehead was touching the ground.

To end the raka'ah, Muslims sit back on their heels and recite Surah 2:255 (known as the verse of the chair because Muslims sit back when they recite it) and then say, "The peace of Allah be with you. The peace and the mercy of Allah be with you."

COMPLETING THE PRAYERS

I have just described one complete raka'ah. For the third prayer of the day, four raka'ahs were required. Each raka'ah would be exactly the same, except for the part in the first half where each person recites his own selection of verses from the Quran.

After the required prayers are finished, most people leave the mosque to continue their activity on campus. However, some stay behind and do extra prayers to show their devotion to Allah.

For thirty years I did these prayers—that's 54,750 prayer times. Many devoted Muslims around the world do these prayers their entire lives. Obviously, this requires discipline and commitment. What motivates a Muslim to persevere in the prayers?

MUHAMMAD'S COMMANDS REGARDING PRAYER

Prayer in Islam is a duty—not an option. Muhammad taught that five prayers a day are a requirement of Allah. Muhammad said that one night in a dream the angel Gabriel took him to see Allah in heaven. (This is referred to as the Night Journey). Allah told Muhammad that people were required to offer prayer fifty times a day. Muhammad said he negotiated with Allah until the requirement was brought down to five.[1] From that time on, Muhammad led the Muslims in prayer five times a day.

These five times are based on the time of sunrise so they vary according to the season.[2] They are:

Prayer	Approximate Time	# of Raka'ahs
First (*Sobh*)	4 a.m.	2
Second (*Dhuhr*)	12 p.m.	4
Third (*Asr*)	3 p.m.	4
Fourth (*Maghrib*)	5 p.m.	3
Fifth (*Isha*)	8:30 p.m.	4

Muhammad said that the angel Gabriel taught him the correct pattern for prayer, so his followers watched him carefully and recorded every detail. Muhammad himself also gave many teachings about the correct way to do prayer in various circumstances. For example, when you don't have water for the washing, you can use sand or dust (Surah 4:43; 5:6). If you are too far away from a mosque to reach it by prayer time, you can use a prayer rug. If you are in the middle of jihad, you may modify your prayers so that you are not vulnerable to enemies while you are praying (Surah 4:101–103).

Muhammad was stern with his followers to make sure they came out for prayers. One time Muhammad had started the evening prayer, and many Muslims were missing. Muhammad asked, "Where is so and so, and so and so, and so and so?"

The reply was, "They are still in their houses."

Muhammad responded:

> By Him in Whose Hand my soul is I was about to order for collecting fire-wood (fuel) and then order Someone to pronounce the Adhan for the prayer and then order someone to lead the prayer then I would go from behind and burn the houses of men who did not present themselves for the (compulsory congregational) prayer.[3]

As you would expect, Muslims struggled with doing the first prayer of the day before sunrise. They wanted to sleep. One hadith records:

> It was mentioned before the Prophet that there was a man who slept the night till morning (after sunrise). The Prophet said, "He is a man in whose ears (or ear) Satan had urinated."[4]

Muhammad taught that if a person refused to do the five prayers he was no longer a Muslim. He explained, "The covenant between us and them is the prayer, and the one who leaves the prayer will be converted."[5]

THE GOAL OF ISLAMIC PRAYER

What do Muslims hope to achieve through prayer?

1. First and foremost, Muslims want to avoid Allah's punishment for disobeying the command to pray five times a day. All that is good comes from Allah, so if he is displeased with you, he can withhold good things from your life, such as taking away your health or hurting your finances or cursing you. If you don't do your prayers, Allah will also punish you on Judgment Day.

2. Second, Muslims hope to please Allah so that he will accept them on Judgment Day and admit them into paradise.

Muslims believe that Allah watches their prayers closely, which is why they are so careful to follow the instructions about how they are to be performed. However, they cannot find out whether Allah was pleased with their prayers (and other good deeds) until Judgment Day.

EXTRA PRAYERS

So far we have learned in detail about the scripted prayer that Muhammad required Muslims to pray five times a day (known in Arabic as *fard* prayer). Muslims may also offer extra voluntary prayers (*nephil* prayers). These can be in the form of extra raka'ahs, which are permitted during specific periods of the day.[6]

It is important to note that all of these prayers are scripted prayers. They must be performed according to specific guidelines. You cannot just say a raka'ah in the car or while you are sitting on the riverbank.

Personal prayers are a different matter. A personal prayer is when a person expresses individual ideas or requests to Allah in whatever way he desires. Personal prayers are not forbidden in Islam, but they are not encouraged or talked about very much. Only a small sect, the Sufites, focus on personal prayer as a way of personal communication with God. The normal Muslim does not expect God to communicate with him personally through prayer.

In Islamic teaching, Allah does not speak to people directly: it is the angel Gabriel who speaks on his behalf. The angel Gabriel is called the Holy Spirit, but he is not considered a part of God and he can only be in one place at one time. (See Surah 2:97–98; 26:193; 16:102.) So when a Muslim prays, he does not expect Allah to communicate with him, nor does he expect Gabriel to come and speak to him.

A Muslim's only hope of hearing from Allah comes on the final night of Ramadan each year. Muhammad taught that on this night Gabriel would visit one person who was pious and waiting for him (Surah 97:4). During this night each year, I and other devoted

Muslims would stay up all night in the mosque with the desire of being visited by Gabriel.

The Bible's teaching about the Holy Spirit is very different. The Bible says the Holy Spirit is a part of the divine Trinity and therefore has the ability to be present in all places at once. This means God, through the Holy Spirit, can communicate with many people at the same time.

Now let's look at prayer as Jesus taught.

JESUS TEACHES HIS FOLLOWERS HOW TO PRAY

As you know, the first time I ever read a Bible, I started reading in Matthew 5. It wasn't long before I came to Matthew 6, where Jesus taught his disciples how to pray. Over and over as I read I saw the contrast between Jesus and Muhammad. Let's look at this passage together:

> And when you pray, do not be like the hypocrites, for they love to pray standing in the synagogues and on the street corners to be seen by men. I tell you the truth, they have received their reward in full. But when you pray, go into your room, close the door and pray to your Father, who is unseen. Then your Father, who sees what is done in secret, will reward you.
>
> —MATTHEW 6:5–6

The first thing I noticed about this passage was the word *when*. This word *when* was like a tornado in my brain. I thought, *This means it's up to me when I pray. I can pray at any time!*

Next I noticed what Jesus said about *where* to pray. He said, "Go to your room and close the door." I thought, *I don't go to the mosque any more?*

Jesus said that God rewards the person who prays alone more than the one who prays so that people will see him. This was the opposite of what Muhammad taught. Muhammad wanted the people to come out of their houses and be together in the mosque for prayer. He said that praying alone was inferior.

> Ibn 'Umar reported Allah's Apostle as saying: The
> prayer of a person in congregation is twenty-seven
> times in excess to the prayer said alone.[7]

Jesus went on to say:

> And when you pray, do not keep on babbling like
> pagans, for they think they will be heard because of
> their many words.
>
> —MATTHEW 6:7

My prayers in Islam were all about "many words." I had to recite certain words and make certain movements many times each day, each week, each year. I believed that Allah required many words in order to be pleased.

> Do not be like them, for your Father knows what you
> need before you ask him.
>
> —MATTHEW 6:8; SEE ALSO VERSES 25–29

Jesus said here that God knew about my needs. He cared about me personally.

Next Jesus gave a sample prayer. (See Matthew 6:9–13.) I had to stop after the first two words:

> Our Father...

I would never pray that way as a Muslim. The Quran taught that God never had a son. As the evening went on, however, I decided that "our Father" was a good thing. I thought, "If God is my father, then I am his son, and between father and son there is nothing such as threats or manipulation. When you talk to your father, you are not afraid, wondering if he will be offended with how you pray."

Then I continued reading:

> Our Father in heaven,
> hallowed be your name,
> your kingdom come,
> your will be done
> on earth as it is in heaven.

This kind of worship sounded natural to me. "Let your name be holy" was a phrase that we used in Islam. However, "your kingdom come" was a new phrase to me. Later I could see that Jesus was setting up a spiritual kingdom, not a political one.

> Give us this day, our daily bread.

When I read this sentence I imagined a little child sitting in front of his dad, asking him for some food. The raka'ah did not include anything about asking Allah to care for me. I am permitted to ask Allah to provide for my needs, but when I do this I am bowed over with my forehead on the floor in submission.

> Forgive us our debts,
> as we also have forgiven our debtors.

Here I had a little stumbling block. I wondered, *Why does Jesus say I must forgive others in order for him to forgive me?* I was worried that this sentence would take me back to Islamic law—working for favor from God. Later I understood that God requires people to forgive others because he forgives first. (See Matthew 18:21–35, the story of the unmerciful servant.)

> And lead us not into temptation,
> but deliver us from the evil one.

The Bible picture showed me that temptation comes from Satan and that God would help us resist it. In Islamic teaching, temptation may come from Satan or temptation may come from Allah who uses demons to lead people astray so that they will populate hell. So I was very impacted by the idea that God is always willing to deliver people from temptation if they ask for help.

This was the end of the Lord's Prayer as recorded in Matthew. By this point I was completely engrossed in reading the Bible. I was so hooked, that I kept reading through the New Testament most of the night. After a few hours I came to Luke 11, which also describes the Lord's Prayer. Luke recorded Jesus' teaching about how God responds to prayers:

> Which of you fathers, if your son asks for a fish, will
> give him a snake instead? Or if he asks for an egg, will
> give him a scorpion? If you then, though you are evil,
> know how to give good gifts to your children, how
> much more will your Father in heaven give the Holy
> Spirit to those who ask him!
>
> —Luke 11:11–13

Again I saw the picture of Father God caring for his children. This was so different from the attitude of Allah, who made his slaves wait until Judgment Day to find out whether he accepted their prayers.

Jesus' Example of Prayer

Jesus gave his disciples a sample prayer, and he also demonstrated prayer in his own life. As I read through the New Testament, I noticed the times where it said that Jesus prayed.

> Very early in the morning, while it was still dark, Jesus
> got up, left the house and went off to a solitary place,
> where he prayed.
>
> —Mark 1:35; see also Mark 6:46
>
> Jesus often withdrew to lonely places and prayed.
>
> —Luke 5:16
>
> One of those days Jesus went out to a mountainside to
> pray, and spent the night praying to God.
>
> —Luke 6:12

Jesus usually prayed alone, but sometimes he took his disciples with him (Luke 9:28; 22:39). However, Jesus never required his disciples to pray at a specific time or in a specific way. He never talked about God punishing them for not praying enough.

The purpose of prayer to Father God

According to what I read in the Gospels, Jesus used prayer as a way to be in communication with God, not as a way to please God.

He taught his disciples to worship God in prayer and to present their needs to him.

We can look at the Book of Acts in the Bible and see how the disciples followed these instructions. The Book of Acts does not speak of Christians repeating the Lord's Prayer verbatim. But it does describe the Christians offering prayers regularly and asking God for help in time of trouble. Acts 4 gives a good example of a prayer, offered when the Christians were being threatened by the chief priests and elders.

> "Sovereign Lord," they said, "you made the heaven and the earth and the sea, and everything in them. Stretch out your hand to heal and perform miraculous signs and wonders through the name of your holy servant Jesus." After they prayed, the place where they were meeting was shaken. And they were all filled with the Holy Spirit and spoke the word of God boldly.
>
> —Acts 4:24, 30–31

THE FUNDAMENTAL DIFFERENCE

The difference in prayer between Jesus and Muhammad is really based in the difference between their understanding of God.

Muhammad described Allah as the master and people as his slaves; therefore, prayer was a way to win favor from the master. If prayers were not performed correctly, the master would be angry. So that is why devoted Muslims spend hours and hours repeating the same words and gestures, day after day, hoping to please Allah.

Jesus pictured God as a Father and people as his children; therefore, prayer was a way to communicate with the one who loved and cared for you. If Christians do not pray, they deprive themselves of the opportunity to communicate with God.

Conclusion

Thus far in this section of the book we have looked at the legacy Jesus and Muhammad left behind:

- Their messages to the world
- Their teaching about each other
- Healings and miracles
- The meaning of holy war
- Teachings about love
- Teachings on prayer

There is one more topic of great interest to modern people that we must address—the treatment of women. The next chapter will look at exactly what Jesus and Muhammad taught about women and how they treated the women with whom they came in contact.

16

Attitudes Toward Women

E ven as a child growing up in Egypt, I chafed at the way Muslim society treated women. As I studied the Quran and Islamic history, I could see how the many restrictions placed upon women came directly from Muhammad himself. Again, this put me in a position of wondering whether the true God of heaven would treat people this way.

My purpose in this chapter is to simply show you Muhammad's attitude toward women and his personal relationships with women in his life. From this you will be able to see how the traditions of Islamic society developed.

We will also look at Jesus' attitude and personal relationships regarding women.

This chapter is divided into three parts:

- Their teachings about women's character
- Their teachings about marriage
- Their personal relationships with women

MUHAMMAD'S TEACHINGS ABOUT WOMEN'S CHARACTER

We have a tremendous amount of information about women both in the Quran and in the teachings of Muhammad recorded in the hadith.

Muhammad makes clear distinctions between women and men. Unfortunately, many of his comments about women are unflattering.

Are women evil?

When Muhammad visited paradise and hell (during the Night Journey), he reported:

> The Prophet said, "I looked into Paradise and found that the majority of its dwellers were the poor people, and I looked into the (Hell) Fire and found that the majority of its dwellers were women."[1]

In Muhammad's day, women had to be careful not to walk by men who were praying.[2] That's because Muhammad said that if a woman walked by a man who was praying, his prayer would be cancelled out and he would have to start his time of prayer from the beginning again. Muhammad's second wife, Aisha, reported this teaching, along with a mild protest:

> The things which annul the prayers were mentioned before me. They said, "Prayer is annulled by a dog, a donkey and a woman (if they pass in front of the praying people)." I said, "You have made us (i.e. women) dogs."[3]

At another time Muhammad described women as an "evil omen" or bad luck.

> Evil omen was mentioned before the Prophet: The Prophet said, "If there is evil omen in anything, it is in the house, the woman and the horse."[4]

Women were considered impure during the time of their periods (menses), and Muhammad said they could not pray or fast on those days. Muhammad said this also put women in a negative position in Allah's eyes.

> Once Allah's Apostle went out to the Musalla (to offer the prayer)....Then he passed by the women and said, "O women! Give alms, as I have seen that the majority of the dwellers of Hell-fire were you (women)." They asked, "Why is it so, O Allah's Apostle?" He replied,

"You curse frequently and are ungrateful to your husbands. I have not seen anyone more deficient in intelligence and religion than you. A cautious sensible man could be led astray by some of you." The women asked, "O Allah's Apostle! What is deficient in our intelligence and religion?" He said, "Is not the evidence of two women equal to the witness of one man?" They replied in the affirmative. He said, "This is the deficiency in her intelligence. Isn't it true that a woman can neither pray nor fast during her menses?" The women replied in the affirmative. He said, "This is the deficiency in her religion."[5]

Are women inferior?

Did Muhammad believe that women are inferior to men? The Quran says that it takes the witness of two women to equal the witness of one man:

Get witnesses out of your own men. And if there are not two men (available), then a man and two women, such as you agree for witnesses, so that if one of them (two women) errs, the other can remind her.

—SURAH 2:282

Muhammad explained the reason for this teaching this way:

The Prophet said, "Isn't the witness of a woman equal to half of that of a man?" The women said, "Yes." He said, "This is because of the deficiency of a woman's mind."[6]

Women also received a smaller share of inheritance than men.

Allah commands you as regards your children's (inheritance): to the male, a portion equal to that of two females.

—SURAH 4:11

Women required to be covered

Many people have questions about the covering for Muslim women. In the beginning of Islam, when Muhammad was living

169

in Mecca with only his first wife, he did not ask Muslim women to wear veils. After moving to Medina, something happened that prompted a new revelation regarding women.

Muhammad began to marry multiple wives, and Muhammad typically hosted a feast after each wedding. After the feast for Zainab bint Jahsh (I will tell you more about her later), several people lingered in his house after Muhammad left.[7]

The next day one of Muhammad's most trusted followers made this suggestion:

> Narrated Umar: I said, "O Allah's Apostle! Good and bad persons enter upon you, so I suggest that you order the mothers of the Believers (i.e. your wives) to observe veils." Then Allah revealed the Verses of Al-Hijab.[8]

That same day Muhammad received revelation through the angel Gabriel that Muslim women should wear veils.

> O Prophet! Tell your wives and your daughters and the women of the believers to draw their cloaks (veils) all over their bodies....That will be better, that they should be known (as free respectable women) so as not to be annoyed.
>
> —SURAH 33:59;
> SEE ALSO VERSE 33 AND SURAH 24:31, 58FF

So women began to cover themselves. Muhammad's second wife, Aisha, commented on how the women followed this new revelation:

> Aisha used to say: "When (the Verse): 'They should draw their veils over their necks and bosoms,' was revealed, (the ladies) cut their waist sheets at the edges and covered their faces with the cut pieces."[9]

So Muhammad's intention regarding the *hijab* was clear, and the Muslim women of his day covered their faces. Conservative Muslims today follow the Quran literally, and the women also cover their faces. Liberal Muslims choose to wear modern, but modest, clothing rather than a full covering.

Women as spoils of war

Whenever a village or tribe resisted Muhammad and his army and they were conquered, the Muslims had permission to take the women and children as slaves. Chapter 29 in book 8 of the hadith of Muslim actually has the following title:

> It is permissible to have sexual intercourse with a captive woman after she is purified (of menses or delivery). In case she has a husband, her marriage is abrogated after she becomes captive.

The hadith goes on to explain when this ruling was made.

> At the Battle of Hanain Allah's Messenger sent an army to Autas and encountered the enemy and fought with them. Having overcome them and taken them captives, the Companions of Allah's Messenger seemed to refrain from having intercourse with captive women because of their husbands being polytheists. Then Allah, Most High, sent down regarding that: "And women already married, except those whom your right hands possess (iv. 24)" (i.e. they were lawful for them when their *Idda* period came to an end).[10]

Not only do hadith contain this ruling, but the Quran itself also makes reference to captive women being at the disposal of their masters, even if they were currently married (Surah 4:24).

Muslims had the option to release the women from slavery and take them as wives if they chose to do so.

Muhammad's care for women

Despite some of his comments and actions toward women, Muhammad also made sure that Muslim women were taken care of, especially the poor and the widowed. (The Islamic community had a significant number of widows due to the practice of jihad.)

He supported them from the spoils of war and the charity tax (*zakat*) that he collected from all people under Islamic authority.

JESUS' TEACHING ABOUT WOMEN'S CHARACTER

Jesus did not make any specific comments about the character of women being different than the character of men. However, we can learn about his attitude toward women by seeing how he treated them. The Gospels describe Jesus praising women for their faith, healing their illnesses, casting out their demons, and forgiving their sins—just as he did for men.

Praising women's faith and healing them

A woman who had been bleeding for twelve years saw Jesus in a crowd. She touched the edge of Jesus' cloak, and he felt it. "Who touched me?" he asked. Trembling with fear, the woman knelt at his feet and told him what she did. She was afraid because according to Jewish law her bleeding made her unclean and she should not touch anyone. Jesus said to her, "Daughter, your faith has healed you. Go in peace and be freed from your suffering" (Mark 5:21–34).

So Jesus praised her faith. His comment stands in contrast to Muhammad's teaching that women are "deficient in religion."

Jesus also praised another woman for her faith. This was a Gentile who persistently begged him to cast the demons out of her daughter. Jesus told her, "Woman, you have great faith! Your request is granted" (Matt.15:28).

Jesus even said that a widow's offering could be more valuable than a rich man's offering.

> As he looked up, Jesus saw the rich putting their gifts into the temple treasury. He also saw a poor widow put in two very small copper coins. "I tell you the truth," he said, "this poor widow has put in more than all the others. All these people gave their gifts out of their wealth; but she out of her poverty put in all she had to live on."
>
> —LUKE 21:1–4

Jesus' attitude contrasts sharply with Muhammad. Remember that Muhammad urged a group of women to "give alms" to make up for their deficiency in intelligence and religion.

Casting out their demons

Some of Jesus' followers were women whom he had delivered from demons.

> The Twelve were with him, and also some women who had been cured of evil spirits and diseases: Mary (called Magdalene) from whom seven demons had come out; Joanna the wife of Cuza, the manager of Herod's household; Susanna; and many others.
> —Luke 8:1–3

Jesus also healed a woman who had been crippled for eighteen years because of a demon (Luke 13:10–13).

Forgiving women's sins

As Jesus and his disciples were traveling through Samaria, they stopped at a well outside of a city. Jesus was tired and rested there while the disciples went into town to buy food. A woman came to draw water, and Jesus began to talk with her. The fact that Jesus talked with her was remarkable in two ways: (1) she was a woman, and (2) she was Samaritan, who were considered impure by the Jews.

After a while, Jesus surprised her by gently pointing out that she was living with a man who wasn't her husband. Amazed that Jesus knew about her life, the woman ran into town and told everyone about him. Jesus stayed there to teach them for two days, and her testimony encouraged many Samaritans to believe on him (John 4:1–42).

Instead of condemning the woman for her sin, Jesus gave her the opportunity to follow him.

Jesus was approached by another woman as he was eating a meal in the home of some religious leaders. A woman who was known for her sinful life entered the house and threw herself at

Jesus' feet, sobbing. As her tears flowed, she washed his feet and dried them with her hair. Then she took an expensive bottle of perfume and anointed his feet with it. The religious leaders whispered, "If this man were a prophet, he would know this woman is a sinner."

Jesus responded by saying, "Yes, this woman has sinned much, but her love for me is great as a result." Jesus said to the woman, "Your sins are forgiven" (Luke 7:36–50).

Jesus also intervened in the case of a woman who had been caught in adultery and was about to be stoned by the religious leaders. Jesus told her accusers: Let he who is without sin cast the first stone. When they all left, Jesus said to her, "Neither do I condemn you....Go now and leave your life of sin" (John 8:11).

MARRIAGE

Muhammad's teaching on women in marriage

Keeping in line with his general attitude toward women, Muhammad described a marriage relationship where the man was superior and the woman needed to be submissive. Regarding the husband, the Quran says:

> Men are the protectors and maintainers of women, because Allah has made one of them to excel the other, and because they spend (to support them) from their means.
>
> —SURAH 4:34

In the same verse, the Quran says regarding the wife:

> Therefore the righteous women are devoutly obedient (to Allah and to their husbands), and guard...(e.g., their chastity, their husband's property).

The second half of this verse gives the husband liberty to punish the wife for bad behavior:

> As to those women on whose part you see ill-conduct, admonish them (first), (next), refuse to share their

beds, (and last) beat them (lightly, if it is useful); but if they return to obedience, seek not against them means (of annoyance).

Women were cursed if they refused to sleep with their husbands:

> The Prophet said, "If a man invites his wife to sleep with him and she refuses to come to him, then the angels send their curses on her till morning."[11]

Divorce was accepted as a part of life in Islamic culture. A man could divorce his wife by saying three times, "I divorce you."[12] But he can choose to marry her again. However, if he also says, "You are like my mother to me," then this is a permanent divorce and he cannot marry her again unless she marries another man and is divorced from him. After that second divorce occurs, the first husband is free to marry her again if he wants (Surah 2:226–232). However, a wife was not permitted to initiate a divorce nor could she stop her husband from divorcing her. (This practice is based on Surah 4:34.)

In the Islamic world today, where Islamic law is being applied, women still are not permitted to initiate or resist a divorce (in countries such as Saudi Arabia, Iran, and Sudan). More secular countries, however, are giving women divorce rights. For example, Egypt passed a law in 2003 permitting women to ask for divorce under specific conditions, such as a husband's infidelity.

Many different scenarios for divorce, compensation, and the waiting period before remarriage are described in the hadith. Islamic law allows divorce under many circumstances, even for very small things. It is up to the attitude of her husband. He can divorce his wife just for being difficult to live with.

The Quran allows a man to have up to four wives if he is able to support them.

> And if you fear that you shall not be able to deal justly with the orphan-girls then marry (other) women of your choice, two, or three, or four.
>
> —SURAH 4:3

Muhammad, however, was permitted to have more than four wives, as you will see later in this chapter.

Jesus' teaching on women in marriage

In contrast to Muhammad, Jesus taught that divorce should be restricted.

> Some Pharisees came and tested him by asking, "Is it lawful for a man to divorce his wife?"
>
> "What did Moses command you?" he replied.
>
> They said, "Moses permitted a man to write a certificate of divorce and send her away."
>
> "It was because your hearts were hard that Moses wrote you this law," Jesus replied. "But at the beginning of creation God 'made them male and female.' 'For this reason a man will leave his father and mother and be united to his wife, and the two will become one flesh.' So they are no longer two, but one. Therefore what God has joined together, let man not separate."
>
> When they were in the house again, the disciples asked Jesus about this. He answered, "Anyone who divorces his wife and marries another woman commits adultery against her. And if she divorces her husband and marries another man, she commits adultery."
>
> —MARK 10:2–12

Jesus gave marriage a high spiritual status. Jesus supported the teachings of the Old Testament that say God ordains the bond between a man and a wife. This bond is so close that it is described as two people becoming one flesh (Gen. 2:24).

Jesus did not give any other specific teaching about marriage. However, his followers did make further comments regarding marriage and divorce, which are recorded in the New Testament.

Now let's look at the role of marriage in the personal lives of Jesus and Muhammad.

MUHAMMAD'S MOST FAMOUS WIVES

Just as Muhammad's attitude toward nonbelievers changed after he moved to Medina, so did his practice regarding wives. Let's look at his first wife and then at the twelve other women he married in Medina.

Khadija, the first wife

When Muhammad was a young man of twenty-five, he married his first wife, Khadija, who was forty at the time. She is described as offering him great emotional support as he received revelations and experienced resistance from the people of Mecca. He remained married to her alone for twenty-five years until her death.

Aisha, the child bride

About one year after moving to Medina, Muhammad chose a wife that was surprising even by Arabian society standards. She was the six-year-old daughter of one of his most loyal followers, Abu Bakr.

> The Prophet wrote the (marriage contract) with Aisha while she was six years old and consummated his marriage with her while she was nine years old and she remained with him for nine years (i.e. till his death).[13]

More than just a perplexing story about a child bride, Aisha became a key figure in Islamic history. She narrated thousands of hadith describing Muhammad's life and teachings. She was also involved in an incident that seriously threatened the credibility of Islam.

When Muhammad led his army in a battle, he always chose one of his wives to go with him. In A.H. 5 he took Aisha with him on a raid against beni Mustaliq, a Jewish tribe. She would have been about eleven years old at that time.

This is the story according to Aisha. Aisha rode in a special covered compartment on the back of a camel. At night the raiding party stopped, and Aisha left the group to use the toilet in the desert. On her way back she realized she had lost her necklace and went back to look for it. By the time she returned to the stopping place, everyone had left, thinking she was in the riding compartment on the camel's back. She waited in the desert until a Muslim soldier came by and recognized her. He brought her back to Medina the next morning on his camel.[14]

Some people accused Aisha of having an affair in the desert with the young Muslim soldier. Muhammad was unable to prove that she did not. People began to say, "How can this man be a prophet if he doesn't know what happened to his wife?" For more than twenty days this standoff continued. Finally Muhammad received a revelation from Gabriel that cleared Aisha of wrongdoing and condemned those who had been accusing her (Surah 42:11–18).

The repercussions of this incident did not end here. One of Muhammad's cousins with whom he grew up, Ali ibn Abu Talib, had urged Muhammad to divorce Aisha. Aisha heard this and carried a grudge against Ali for the rest of her life. After the death of the third leader of Islam (Uthman), Ali ibn Abu Talib was elected to become the next Islamic calipha. But Aisha refused to recognize him as the leader, and she gathered an army of supporters and marched against him. In the ensuing Battle of Camel, ten thousand Muslims were killed. Ali ibn Abu Talib was killed, and his son became his successor until he was poisoned by Muslims.

So Aisha, the child bride, is a major figure in Islamic history. Let's look at another one of Muhammad's most interesting wives.

Zainab, the wife of Muhammad's adopted son

Muhammad went one day to the house of his adopted son Zaid Bin Harithah. When he arrived, he found out that his adopted son wasn't home, and that his son's wife, Zainab, was home alone. As she came to the door, his eyes met hers, and Muhammad said, "Praise be to the one who changes the hearts and the sights." He felt her love in his heart. She became aware that he had a certain desire for her. When her husband came back, she told him what had happened. There were two problems with this situation. First, Zainab was married, and second, her husband was Muhammad's adopted son. Islamic law forbid a man from marrying his son's wives.

However, from that day on, Zainab mistreated her husband by showing him she was not interested in him any longer. Every time she would do so, Zaid would go to Muhammad and complain about his wife and tell him about the abuse he was getting from her. And every time Muhammad would tell him, "Keep your wife to yourself, and fear Allah" (Surah 33:37).

After this continued for a while, Zaid apparently gave up on the marriage and divorced his wife.

Islamic history says that Muhammad then decided to ask Zainab to marry him, even though this defied Islamic law about a man marrying his son's wives. Oddly, Muhammad sent Zaid to deliver the proposal. Zaid went to his ex-wife's house and found her preparing flour to make bread. Zaid said of the moment, "When I saw her, I could not even look on her face because I still loved her." But he dutifully delivered the message from Muhammad. His ex-wife replied, "Allah must tell me to marry him." She told Zaid that she was going to the mosque to pray. So Zaid went back to Muhammad and told him what had happened.[15]

While Zainab was still at the mosque, Muhammad reported a new revelation from the angel Gabriel.

> Behold! you said to one who had received the grace of Allah and your favor: "You retain (in wedlock) your wife, and fear Allah." But you hid in your heart that which Allah was about to make manifest: you feared the people, but it is more fitting that you should fear Allah. Then when Zaid had dissolved (his marriage) with her, with the necessary (formality), We joined her in marriage to your: in order that (in future) there may be no difficulty to the Believers in (the matter of) marriage with the wives of their adopted sons, when the latter have dissolved with the necessary (formality) (their marriage) with them. And

> Allah's command must be fulfilled.
> There can be no difficulty to the Prophet in what
> Allah has indicated to him as a duty.
> —SURAH 33:37–38, ALI TRANSLATION

This revelation specifically said that Allah commanded Zainab to be married to Muhammad. The verse also pointed out that this marriage would help other Muslims by showing them that it was permissible for a man to marry his adopted son's former wife if the marriage had been properly dissolved.

Muhammad also received a revelation that abolished adoption. "Allah has not...made your adopted sons your real sons" (Surah 33:4). As a result, Zaid was no longer considered Muhammad's son, which also served to legalize Muhammad's marriage to Zainab.

In the end, Zainab agreed to marry Muhammad and became his fifth wife (A.H. 5). Her former husband died three years later while fighting in jihad.

Zainab was quite happy with how things turned out for her. The hadith record:

> Zainab used to boast before the wives of the Prophet
> and used to say, "You were given in marriage by your
> families, while I was married (to the Prophet) by Allah
> from over seven Heavens."[16]

Let's look at one more specific example of how Muhammad obtained one of his wives—this one as a prisoner of war.

Safiya, the Jewish beauty

By A.H. 7 Muhammad had already routed most of the Jews out of Arabia. There was one village remaining—Khaybar. Muhammad and his army surrounded the village at night and attacked while the people were still asleep. He killed most of the young men and adults, and the women and children were taken as prisoners.[17]

Muhammad noticed one of the prisoners, a beautiful girl named Safiya. Her father was the leader of Khaybar, and she was still a new bride. Both her husband and father were killed by the Muslims that day. Muhammad asked his men, "Whose prisoner is that woman?" They replied, "She belongs to Qais bin Thabet Al-Shammas."

Muhammad gave this man Safiya's two cousins and took Safiya for himself. She traveled with Muhammad back toward Medina. During the journey, after her period (menses) was over, Muhammad married her.[18]

The night Muhammad consummated his marriage with Safiya, one of Muhammad's followers stayed up all night walking around the tent with his sword at his side. In the morning Muhammad asked him why he did this. The man replied, "I was afraid for you with this woman for you have killed her father, her husband, and her people, and till recently she was in unbelief, so I was afraid for you on her account."[19]

MUHAMMAD'S OTHER WIVES

Each of Muhammad's wives had a story behind her, and I have told you the most significant and interesting ones. The complete listing of wives is as follows:[20]

1. Khadija bint Khu-walid (He was married to her in Mecca for twenty-five years until her death.)

2. Aisha bint Abu Bakr (She was young, jealous, and caused trouble, but she was the favored one, daughter of Muhammad's closest friend, and first successor to Islam.)

3. Hafza bint Umar ibn al-Khattab (She was the daughter of one of Muhammad's fiercest warriors.)

4. Umm-Habib Rumleh bint Abi Sufyan (She was the daughter of the leader of Quraysh tribe in Mecca who converted to Islam just before Muhammad conquered the city.)

5. Zainab bint Jahsh (She was first the wife of Muhammad's adopted son. They divorced and Muhammad married her.)

6. Umm Salama Hend bint Abi Ummayah

7. Maymuna bint el-Harith al-Hilleliah

8. Sauda bint Zema'a el Amawiya

9. Juwayriya bint al-Harith (She was a Jewish girl taken as a prisoner of war in the raid on beni Mustaliq, which incidentally was the same raid during which Aisha was accused of adultery.)

10. Safiya bint Ho-yay (She was a Jewish girl taken as a prisoner of war during the raid on Khaybar.)

11. Ra-hana bint Shumahon

12. Maria bint Shumahon

13. Umm Sharik

As you remember, the Quran only allowed Muslims two, three, or four wives, but Muhammad was an exception. Muhammad reported a revelation that defined the women he was permitted to marry:

> O Prophet! We have made lawful to you your wives to whom you have paid their dowers; and those whom your right hand possesses out of the prisoners of war whom Allah has assigned to you; and daughters of your paternal uncles and aunts, and daughters of your maternal uncles and aunts, who migrated (from Makkah) with you; and any believing woman who dedicates her soul to the Prophet if the Prophet wishes to wed her; - this only for you, and not for the Believers (at large).
>
> —SURAH 33:50, ALI TRANSLATION

When Muhammad died he left nine living widows. Muhammad prohibited any of them from remarrying after his death (Surah 33:6, 52).

Muhammad's other women

In addition to his wives, Muhammad had another group of women at his disposal. These were the female slaves whom he had purchased or acquired as prisoners of war. All slaves, whether male or female, were referred to in Arabic as *milkelimen*. The male slaves would serve Muhammad by doing chores such as taking care of Muhammad and his wives, their houses, and their animals. They would prepare food and bring the water for washing before prayers. Forty-three of these male slaves are listed by name in Islamic history.[21]

The female slaves performed chores as well, but Islamic law also permitted Muhammad to use them sexually without being required to marry them. Any resulting child would not carry the name of Muhammad or take any inheritance from him. The child would be a slave to Muhammad, not his son, and Muhammad had the right to keep him or to sell him. (Islamic law allowed *milkelimen* for any Muslim man). Twenty three of these female slaves are listed by name in Islamic history.[22]

MUHAMMAD'S GENERAL RELATIONSHIP WITH HIS WIVES

Muhammad's social life was always full of struggles between him and his wives and among the wives themselves. Islamic history records many details about these skirmishes. One time Muhammad's wives were persistently asking Muhammad for money, and he said that he had none to give them. In exasperation, he separated himself from them for one month (twenty-nine days). Then he offered each of his wives the option to be divorced from him. He told Aisha, his child bride, that she may want to consult her parents in this matter. All the wives conceded to remain in his household.[23]

In order to manage his relationships with his wives, Muhammad assigned each wife a day to spend with him. But when Aisha caused him trouble, he would take another wife's day and spend it with her. One wife complained about this situation, and Muhammad threatened to divorce her. Because she was old she conceded, "Don't divorce me. I will stay with you and give up my night to Aisha."

Jesus and the Women Who Helped Him

There is no record in the Gospels or Christian history that Jesus ever married or had a wife. He is described as having a good relationship with two sisters, Mary and Martha, and he ate meals at their house (Luke 10; John 12).

The Gospel writers also mention that a small group of women traveled with him and the disciples and helped them.

> After this, Jesus traveled about from one town and village to another, proclaiming the good news of the kingdom of God. The Twelve were with him, and also some women who had been cured of evil spirits and diseases: Mary (called Magdalene) from whom seven demons had come out; Joanna the wife of Cuza, the manager of Herod's household; Susanna; and many others. These women were helping to support them out of their own means.
>
> —Luke 8:1–3

These women were loyal followers, and they stayed with Jesus through his crucifixion.

> Many women were there, watching from a distance. They had followed Jesus from Galilee to care for his needs. Among them were Mary Magdalene, Mary the mother of James and Joses, and the mother of Zebedee's sons.
>
> —Matthew 27:55–56

After Jesus' body was removed from the cross, two of the women followed after Joseph of Arimathea and watched as he placed the body in a tomb and rolled a large stone in front of the entrance

(Matt. 27:57–61). Then they went and prepared spices with which to anoint the body after the day of rest (Sabbath) had passed.

These were the women who were the first people to see Jesus after his resurrection.

> After the Sabbath, at dawn on the first day of the week,
> Mary Magdalene and the other Mary went to look at the
> tomb. Suddenly Jesus met them. "Greetings," he said.
> They came to him, clasped his feet and worshiped him.
> Then Jesus said to them, "Do not be afraid. Go and tell
> my brothers to go to Galilee; there they will see me."
> —MATTHEW 28:1, 9–10

So we can see that women followed Jesus and helped him. Jesus even gave women the privilege of being the first to see him after his resurrection. We have no indication that Jesus had sexual relations with them. Jewish society would have condemned such behavior.

CONCLUSION

What have we learned about the attitudes of Jesus and Muhammad toward women?

Women's character. Muhammad described women negatively. Jesus treated women the same way that he treated men.

Teachings about marriage. Muhammad described a relationship where the woman needed to be subject to the man and where it was acceptable for a man to divorce a woman under many circumstances. Jesus spoke of marriage as a union ordained by God that should only be broken by a spouse's unfaithfulness.

Relationships with women. Muhammad had many wives and experienced many challenges with them. Jesus never married but had a group of women who traveled with him and helped him.

Again we see the differences in the personality and character of Jesus and Muhammad. It is especially interesting to observe how these differences play out when they faced similar challenges. The next chapter describes four surprisingly parallel events in their lives and how they responded.

17

Interesting Coincidences

A s I studied the life of Jesus, one of the most interesting experiences for me was discovering unique incidents in his life that
were echoed in the life of Muhammad. In this chapter you will see
how Jesus and Muhammad responded to:

- A woman caught in adultery
- A blind man asking for help
- Followers abandoning them in a time of trouble
- Hungry people in the wilderness

WOMAN GUILTY OF ADULTERY IS JUDGED

Muhammad

> A woman came to Muhammad and said, "I have
> committed adultery, so purify me." [She wanted
> Muhammad to punish her so that Allah would forgive
> her sin and let her into Paradise.] Muhammad told her,
> Go away until you give birth to the child."
>
> After she gave birth, she returned with the child
> and said, "Here is the child I have given birth to."
> Muhammad answered, "Go away and nurse him until
> you wean him."
>
> When she had weaned him, she came to
> Muhammad with the child, who was holding a piece
> of bread in his hand. [The child was probably about
> two years old because that was the length of time

186

the Quran prescribed for nursing.] The woman said, "Allah's Apostle, here is he as I have weaned him and he eats food."

Muhammad gave the child to one of the Muslims and then pronounced punishment. The woman was buried in a ditch up to her chest, and the people stoned her.[1]

This story is used popularly in Islamic preaching as an example of the mercy of Muhammad!

Jesus

The teachers of the law and the Pharisees brought in a woman caught in adultery. They made her stand before the group and said to Jesus, "Teacher, this woman was caught in the act of adultery. In the Law Moses commanded us to stone such women. Now what do you say?" They were using this question as a trap, in order to have a basis for accusing him. But Jesus bent down and started to write on the ground with his finger. When they kept on questioning him, he straightened up and said to them, "If any one of you is without sin, let him be the first to throw a stone at her." Again he stooped down and wrote on the ground. At this, those who heard began to go away one at a time, the older ones first, until only Jesus was left, with the woman still standing there. Jesus straightened up and asked her, "Woman, where are they? Has no one condemned you?" "No one, sir," she said. "Then neither do I condemn you," Jesus declared. "Go now and leave your life of sin."

–JOHN 8:3–11

BLIND MAN ASKS FOR HELP

Muhammad

Some of the most important chiefs from Mecca had come to one of Muhammad's assemblies, and Muhammad was earnestly engaged in persuading them to accept Islam. At this moment a blind man approached him wanting an explanation of some point concerning Islam. Muhammad did not like the interruption and ignored him.[2]

After this incident, Muhammad reported that Allah rebuked him for his attitude toward the blind man (Surah 80:1–15).

> (The Prophet) frowned and turned away. Because there came to him the blind man....And how can you know that he might become pure (from sins)? Or he might receive admonition and the admonition might profit him?
>
> —SURAH 80:1–4

The point to see here is that Muhammad ignored the blind man instead of helping him as he requested.

Jesus

> As Jesus approached Jericho, a blind man was sitting by the roadside begging. When he heard the crowd going by, he asked what was happening. They told him, "Jesus of Nazareth is passing by." He called out, "Jesus, Son of David, have mercy on me!" Those who led the way rebuked him and told him to be quiet, but he shouted all the more, "Son of David, have mercy on me!" Jesus stopped and ordered the man to be brought to him. When he came near, Jesus asked him, "What do you want me to do for you?" "Lord, I want to see," he replied. Jesus said to him, "Receive your sight; your faith has healed you." Immediately he received his sight and followed Jesus, praising God. When all the people saw it, they also praised God.
>
> —LUKE 18:35–43

This blind man saw that Jesus had been healing people, and he asked for help. Jesus gave him what he asked for.

FOLLOWERS RUN AWAY IN TIME OF TROUBLE

Muhammad

After Muhammad conquered Mecca, some of the remaining free people of Arabia joined together in an attempt to defeat him. Leading on his white mule, Muhammad marched out against them with a huge army of twelve thousand men. However, the enemy made a surprise ambush against them in the morning twilight, and Muhammad's soldiers broke rank and fled in terror. Muhammad withdrew to the right and shouted, "Where are you going, men? Come to me. I am God's apostle. I am Muhammad the son of Abdullah." A few stayed with him, but most kept running. Muhammad asked a man with a "powerful voice" who was standing by to call out for the people. One hundred fighters eventually came back to stand with Muhammad. Ultimately the huge Muslim army defeated their enemy that day. This is known as the Battle of Hunayn.[3]

The point is that Muhammad demanded that his followers protect him.

Jesus

> While he was still speaking, Judas, one of the Twelve, arrived. With him was a large crowd armed with swords and clubs, sent from the chief priests and the elders of the people....Then the men stepped forward, seized Jesus and arrested him. With that, one of Jesus' companions reached for his sword, drew it out and struck the servant of the high priest, cutting off his ear. "Put your sword back in its place," Jesus said to him, "for all who draw the sword will die by the sword. Do you think I cannot call on my Father, and he will at once put at my disposal more than twelve legions of angels? But how then would the Scriptures be fulfilled that say it must happen in this way?"....Then all the disciples deserted him and fled.
> —MATTHEW 26:47, 50–54, 56

The point is that Jesus did not allow his disciples to fight for him, and he did not call them back when they ran away.

Hungry in the Desert

Muhammad

The people of Mecca signed an agreement to boycott Muhammad, his clan, and the Muslims, refusing to sell them food.[4] This lasted for two to three years. Eventually Muhammad and the Muslims left the city to go live in the desert valley next to it. They were becoming desperate. Islamic history says Muhammad's people became so hungry they ate the dung of animals and the leaves from trees. This became known as the Year of Hunger.

They survived on supplies brought to them secretly by sympathizers and friends. After a while, the leaders of Mecca decided voluntarily to lift the boycott. Muhammad could not supernaturally supply food for his people during this time.

Jesus

Jesus also encountered a time when his followers were hungry. About five thousand men had followed Jesus into the countryside to hear him teach. They stayed so long that they ate all their food and became hungry. A boy gave Jesus two fish and five loaves of bread. Jesus prayed over the food and asked his disciples to pass it out. It was enough to feed everyone. (See John 6:1–14.)

Conclusion

These parallel incidents provide another way of seeing the differences between Jesus and Muhammad. In the next chapter I will present some parallel teachings. In other words, you can compare the words of Jesus and Muhammad directly on topics such as judging others, revenge, forgiveness, and more.

18

A Comparison of Practical Teachings

Now that you have a thorough background for understanding Jesus and Muhammad, simple verse-by-verse comparisons will have clarity for you. Here is a sample of eight practical teachings.

FORBIDDEN FOOD AND DRINK

Muhammad

Both alcohol and eating pork were forbidden to Muslims (among other things).

> O you who believe! Intoxicants and gambling, (dedication of) stones, and (divination by) arrows, are an abomination—of Satan's handiwork.
>
> —SURAH 5:90, ALI TRANSLATION

> Say "I do not find in the Message received by me by inspiration any (meat) forbidden to be eaten by one who wishes to eat it, unless it be dead meat, or blood poured forth, or the flesh of swine.
>
> —SURAH 6:145, ALI TRANSLATION

Muhammad personally punished some of those who drank wine.

> Anas reported that Allah's Apostle used to strike forty times with shoes and palm branches (in case of drinking of) wine.[1]

Jesus

Jesus did not define righteousness by what a person ate or drank. He said:

> "Don't you see that nothing that enters a man *from the outside* can make him 'unclean'? For it doesn't go into his heart but into his stomach, and then out of his body." (In saying this, Jesus declared all foods "clean.") He went on: "What comes *out of* a man is what makes him 'unclean.' For from within, out of men's hearts, come evil thoughts, sexual immorality, theft, murder, adultery, greed, malice, deceit, lewdness, envy, slander, arrogance and folly. All these evils come from inside and make a man 'unclean.'"
> —MARK 7:18–23, EMPHASIS ADDED

FASTING

Muhammad

Muhammad required Muslims to fast between first prayers (around 4 a.m.) and fourth prayers (around 5 p.m.) during the holy month of Ramadan.

> Ramadhan is the (month) in which was sent down the Qur'an, as a guide to mankind, also clear (Signs) for guidance and judgment (between right and wrong). So every one of you who is present (at his home) during that month should spend it in fasting, but if any one is ill, or on a journey, the prescribed period (should be made up) by days later. Allah intends every facility for you; He does not want to put you to difficulties. (He wants you) to complete the prescribed period, and to glorify Him in that He has guided you; and perchance you shall be grateful.
> —SURAH 2:185, ALI TRANSLATION

Jesus

Jesus did not require his followers to fast.

> Now John's disciples and the Pharisees were fasting. Some people came and asked Jesus, "How is it that John's disciples and the disciples of the Pharisees are fasting, but yours are not?" Jesus answered, "How can the guests of the bridegroom fast while he is with them? They cannot, so long as they have him with them. But the time will come when the bridegroom will be taken from them, and on that day they will fast.
>
> —MARK 2:18–20

Jesus rarely mentioned fasting, with the exception of a time when he said a certain demon would only come out by "prayer and fasting" (Matt. 17:21, NKJV; Mark 9:29, NKJV).

JUDGING OTHERS

Muhammad

If Muslims saw someone breaking Islamic law, Muhammad commanded them to do something about it.

> I heard the Messenger of Allah as saying: He who amongst you sees something abominable should modify it with the help of his hand; and if he has not strength enough to do it, then he should do it with his tongue, and if he has not strength enough to do it, (even) then he should (abhor it) from his heart, and that is the least of faith.[2]

Jesus

Jesus called for his followers to examine themselves instead of looking at how other people behaved.

> Do not judge, or you too will be judged. For in the same way you judge others, you will be judged, and with the measure you use, it will be measured to you. Why do you look at the speck of sawdust in your brother's eye and pay no attention to the plank in your own eye? How can you say to your brother, "Let me take the speck out of your eye," when all the time there

is a plank in your own eye? You hypocrite, first take the plank out of your own eye, and then you will see clearly to remove the speck from your brother's eye.

—MATTHEW 7:1–5

REVENGE

Muhammad

Islamic law is based on al-Ka'saas, which means "eye for eye and tooth for tooth." So let's look to how the Quran defines the relationship between al-Ka'saas and forgiveness. Surah 42:40 says,

> The recompense for an injury is an injury equal thereto (in degree): But if a person forgives and makes reconciliation, his reward is due from God: For God loves not those who do wrong.

However, the verse preceding it (v. 39) instructs the Muslim to practice Al-Ka'saas, "When an oppressive wrong is done to them, take revenge." And the verse following says, "And indeed whosoever takes revenge after he has suffered wrong, for such there is no way (of blame) against them" (v. 41).

In other words, the Quran says forgiveness is best, but eye-for-eye (taking revenge) is still good enough.

Jesus

> You have heard that it was said, "Eye for eye, and tooth for tooth." But I tell you, Do not resist an evil person. If someone strikes you on the right cheek, turn to him the other also. And if someone wants to sue you and take your tunic, let him have your cloak as well. If someone forces you to go one mile, go with him two miles. Give to the one who asks you, and do not turn away from the one who wants to borrow from you.
>
> —MATTHEW 5:38–42

CURSING ENEMIES

Muhammad

Muhammad sometimes cursed people during his prayers. One of the Muslims reported the following story:

> That he heard the Prophet, after raising his head from the bowing in morning prayer, saying, "O Allah, our Lord! All the praises are for you." And in the last (Rak'a) he said, "O Allah! Curse so-and-so and so-and-so."[3]

Jesus

Compare Muhammad's attitude to Jesus' prayer as he was dying on the cross:

> They crucified two robbers with him, one on his right and one on his left. Those who passed by hurled insults at him, shaking their heads and saying, "So! You who are going to destroy the temple and build it in three days, come down from the cross and save yourself!" In the same way the chief priests and the teachers of the law mocked him among themselves. "He saved others," they said, "but he can't save himself! Let this Christ, this King of Israel, come down now from the cross, that we may see and believe." Those crucified with him also heaped insults on him.
> —MARK 15:27–32

> Jesus said, "Father, forgive them, for they do not know what they are doing."
> —LUKE 23:34

FORGIVING THOSE WHO WRONG YOU

Muhammad

> The recompense for an injury is an injury equal thereto (in degree): but if a person forgives and makes reconciliation, his reward is due from Allah: for (Allah) loveth not those who do wrong. But indeed if any do

help and defend themselves after a wrong (done) to them, against such there is no cause of blame. The blame is only against those who oppress men and wrongdoing and insolently transgress beyond bounds through the land, defying right and justice: for such there will be a penalty grievous. But indeed if any show patience and forgive, that would truly be an exercise of courageous will and resolution in the conduct of affairs.

—SURAH 42:40–43, ALI TRANSLATION

Jesus

If someone strikes you on one cheek, turn to him the other also. If someone takes your cloak, do not stop him from taking your tunic. Give to everyone who asks you, and if anyone takes what belongs to you, do not demand it back. Do to others as you would have them do to you. If you love those who love you, what credit is that to you? Even 'sinners' love those who love them. And if you do good to those who are good to you, what credit is that to you? Even 'sinners' do that. And if you lend to those from whom you expect repayment, what credit is that to you? Even 'sinners' lend to 'sinners,' expecting to be repaid in full. But love your enemies, do good to them, and lend to them without expecting to get anything back. Then your reward will be great.

—LUKE 6:29–35

THE SWORD

Muhammad

O Prophet (Muhammad)! Urge the believers to fight. If there are twenty steadfast persons amongst you, they will overcome two hundreds, and if there be a hundred steadfast persons they will overcome a thousand of those who disbelieve, because they (the disbelievers) are people who do not understand.

—SURAH 8:65

Jesus

> Then the men stepped forward, seized Jesus and arrested him. With that, one of Jesus' companions reached for his sword, drew it out and struck the servant of the high priest, cutting off his ear. "Put your sword back in its place," Jesus said to him, "for all who draw the sword will die by the sword.
>
> —MATTHEW 26:50–52

CAPTIVES

Muhammad

> It is not for a Prophet that he should have prisoners of war (and free them with ransom) until he had made a great slaughter (among his enemies) in the land.
>
> —SURAH 8:67

Jesus

> The Spirit of the Lord is upon Me,
>> Because He has anointed Me
> To preach the gospel to the poor;
>> He has sent Me to heal the brokenhearted,
> To proclaim liberty to the *captives*
>> And recovery of sight to the blind,
> To set at liberty those who are oppressed;
>> To proclaim the acceptable year of the LORD.
>> —LUKE 4:18–19, NKJV, EMPHASIS ADDED

CONCLUSION

There are many more comparisons that could be made, but this gives you some good examples. If you continue your study of Jesus and Muhammad, you will discover many more on your own.

This chapter concludes the section of the book titled, "Their Legacy in Words in Deeds." In the last section of this book, I offer a chapter that summarizes all the information you have read thus far, and I use the final chapter to finish my personal story about encountering Jesus and Muhammad side-by-side.

SECTION 4
CONCLUSION

19

Summary of
Key Points

As I promised at the beginning, we have walked together through the lives of Jesus and Muhammad. We have gone through so much information that I think it is important for you to review what you have learned. This chapter will give you a summary of the key points from each chapter.

THEIR LIFE STORIES

Chapter 4: Childhood Destinies
(Birth up to young adult)

Muhammad

Muhammad was born in A.D. 570, almost six hundred years after Jesus. As a child, he spent time at Al-Ka'ba, the Arabian center for idol worship located in Muhammad's hometown of Mecca. Islamic history says that a Nestorian Christian priest prophesied over him when he was twelve. Muhammad began to question the idol worship of his people.

Jesus

Jesus was born around 6/5 B.C. His family was Jewish, so he regularly visited the temple in Jerusalem to observe Jewish holy days. As an infant, he was prophesied over by a priest and a prophetess at the temple. Jesus embraced the faith of his people.

Chapter 5: The Beginning of the Revelations

Muhammad (age 40)

As a young man, Muhammad helped to lead one of Mecca's caravans, and at the age of twenty-five he married Khadija, the owner of the largest caravan. Muhammad visited Al-Ka'ba, but he also spent many days meditating alone in one of the mountain caves around Mecca.

At the age of forty, Muhammad said he was visited by a supernatural being as he was meditating. His wife and her cousin, an Ebionite Christian priest, assured him that he had experienced a message from the true God through the angel Gabriel.

Jesus (age 32 to 33)

As a young man, Jesus lived in Nazareth and probably practiced the trade he learned from Joseph—carpentry. We have no record that he married. He regularly visited the local synagogue and read the Scriptures to the people.

In his early thirties, Jesus presented himself to his cousin, John, who called people to repent of their sins and baptized them in the Jordan River. John baptized Jesus and later declared, "I have seen and testify that this is the Son of God" (John 1:34).

Both Jesus and Muhammad were tested during the first days of their revelations. The Gospels tell of Jesus' overcoming Satan's temptation to sin. The hadith tell of a period when the angel Gabriel stopped appearing to Muhammad, and Muhammad wanted to commit suicide as a result. Gabriel ultimately returned to assure Muhammad that he was a true prophet.

Chapter 6: The People Respond

Muhammad—the first thirteen years in Mecca (age 40 to 53)

For the first three years, Muhammad shared his revelations quietly in Mecca, converting first his wife, then his ten-year-old cousin, followed by a few other people. The leaders of Muhammad's own tribe in Mecca vigorously resisted his new ideas about Allah.

Converts to Islam were harassed or tortured. Ultimately the tribal leaders established a boycott against the Muslims and Muhammad's clan. After two or three years, the tribal leaders chose to lift the boycott voluntarily, yet Muhammad knew he needed protection. He signed an agreement for the two most powerful tribes of Medina to be his protectors. He and all the Muslims moved to Medina when Muhammad was fifty years old. He accepted twelve leaders from these tribes to be his special assistants.

Jesus—the first one to two years of ministry up to the time he sent disciples out to preach without him (age 34)

In contrast, within days of his baptism, Jesus went to the temple in Jerusalem and rebuked the materialism he found there, capturing the attention of all the Jews. He stayed in Jerusalem, teaching and performing miraculous signs (John 2:23). People were attracted to the miracles and the message and began following him. Jesus selected twelve men to be his closest disciples.

Chapter 7: Spreading the Message

Muhammad—the first seven years in Medina (age 53 to 60)

Muhammad's public and private life changed dramatically after his move to Medina. Due to his treaty with the two powerful tribes, he was able to establish a small army and begin conducting raids. They won a major surprise victory against the army of Mecca at the Battle of Badr. After this victory, Muhammad reported revelations from the angel Gabriel commanding all Muslims to fight nonbelievers (Surah 8:39). Most of Muhammad's twelve assistants became military leaders. Each soldier was permitted to keep a percentage of the property that was confiscated from the conquered.

In Medina, Muhammad was living close to the largest Jewish community in Arabia. They rejected his message, and as Muhammad's military strength grew, they recognized him as a threat. Some Jews cooperated with the people of Mecca to organize an unsuccessful attack against Muhammad. In return, Muhammad attacked all the Jewish communities of Arabia and confiscated their property. When he attacked the Jewish tribe of Qurayzah, Muhammad killed all the men (six hundred to nine hundred) and took the women and children captive.

Finally, Muhammad's personal life in Medina was much different than in Mecca. He married twelve women who became a source of stress and conflict in his life.

Jesus—the final one to two years of ministry up to his final journey to Jerusalem (age 34 to 36)

As Jesus entered his third and final year of ministry, he continued to preach the message as before. He accelerated the spread of his message by sending his disciples out to preach in pairs. He instructed them to heal the sick, raise the dead, and cast out demons. They were not permitted to carry money or accept money.

Jesus was a Jew himself, but he was rejected by most of the religious leaders of the Jews, who also plotted ways to kill him. Jesus responded with forceful, verbal rebuttals but no physical attacks.

Regarding Jesus' personal life, the Gospels mention close friendships but they do not describe him ever marrying.

Chapter 8: Last Days

Muhammad—the last three years of his life (age 60 to 63)

During his eighth year in Medina, Muhammad conquered the city of Mecca with superior military force and strategy. He rode his horse through the city streets and took control of Al-Ka'ba in the name of Allah. Muhammad again reported revelations from Gabriel calling for Muslims to fight those who refused to submit to Islamic authority. Most of Arabia's leaders sent messengers to Muhammad saying, "We submit."

In his eleventh year in Medina, Muhammad became seriously ill with a fever. After twenty days of sickness he died in the arms of his wife Aisha.

Summary of Key Points

Jesus—the final months of his life (around age 36)

During the final days of his life, Jesus went to Jerusalem in order to celebrate the Jewish feast of Passover. He rode into the city on a young donkey as crowds of people shouted praises. After he ate the Passover meal, Jesus and his disciples went to a mountain to pray. The Jewish religious leaders arrested him there and put him on trail. He was sentenced to death by crucifixion, and the sentence was carried out. Three days later his disciples reported seeing him alive again, and his body was missing. The Gospels record Jesus' final instructions to his followers, telling them to preach repentance and forgiveness of sins in his name to all nations.

THEIR TEACHINGS

Chapter 10: Their Messages to the World

Muhammad

Muhammad described himself as a prophet who had come to present the true picture of Allah to the world. He specifically taught that he had no power to forgive sins. He said that Islam was the true religion practiced by Abraham but distorted by Jews and Christians. In order to please Allah and enter paradise, a person must follow the teachings of Islam, especially the five pillars. If a person commits a small sin, he can do good deeds to earn forgiveness. But if a person commits a great sin, Allah alone decides if he will forgive. After death, people wait in their graves until Judgment Day. Then each person will go before Allah who will weigh his deeds and decide whether the person goes to paradise or hell.

Jesus

Jesus said he was the son of God and had authority to forgive sins. He described himself as the fulfillment of the law and the prophets of the Jewish Scriptures. At the "end of the age" Jesus said he would judge the living and the dead and send the righteous to heaven and the unrighteous to hell. To enter heaven, a person must believe on Jesus Christ, as evidenced by obedience to his commands.

Chapter 11: Their Teachings About Each Other

Muhammad

Muhammad often mentioned Jesus in his teachings and expressed great respect for him. However, Muhammad always maintained that Jesus was only a prophet of Allah and not the son of God. Even though Muhammad accepted Jesus being born to a virgin, he denied his crucifixion and resurrection. Muhammad condemned Christians for worshiping Jesus as God.

Jesus

Because Jesus lived six hundred years before Muhammad, he did not speak of him directly. However, we can draw come conclusions about what Jesus would have said about Muhammad based on Jesus' other teachings. I suggest that Jesus would have challenged Muhammad's prophethood in three areas: (1) Muhammad's treatment of other people, (2) Muhammad's description of the requirements to please God, and (3) Muhammad's description of the nature of God.

Chapter 12: Healings and Miracles

Healings and miracles are a central part of Jesus' story. But healings and miracles in Muhammad's life are a point of debate among Muslims. Even though the hadith describe some miracles, the Quran denies that Muhammad gave signs, so some Muslims reject the miracle stories. Either way, healings and miracles did not play a large role in Muhammad's life. When you compare the stories regarding Jesus and Muhammad you will see:

1. Regarding healing, there are only a few anecdotes from the life of Muhammad. In Jesus' life, you find his entire ministry revolving around healing people.

2. Regarding casting out demons, I could find no record of Muhammad ever casting out a demon, but the Gospels describe Jesus casting out demons as often as he healed people.

3. Regarding miracles of nature, almost all the supernatural stories told about Muhammad would be categorized as miracles of nature. However, there is no record of these miracles having a strong influence on his followers. The Gospels speak of Jesus performing miracles to effectively support his claims about himself.

Chapter 13: The Meaning of Holy War

Just as healings and miracles were dominant in the life of Jesus, jihad (holy war) played a major role in the life of Muhammad and the spread of Islam. For thirteen years in Mecca, Muhammad practiced tolerance in the face of persecution. But after he put together an army in Medina, he called for holy war against nonbelievers and those who had persecuted him. He promised that Allah would reward Muslims for going to battle. He never stopped calling for holy war up to his death. Despite Muhammad's example, moderate Muslims believe that today holy war should be understood as a struggle within oneself to do good.

Some Muslims point to a handful of references from the New Testament (especially Matt. 10:34) and claim that Jesus called for holy war. However the meaning of these passages based on the context does not support this conclusion. Instead, Jesus consistently refused to fight or defend himself. When threatened he would go away to a safer place. Jesus called on his disciples to practice mercy, peace, and forgiveness, even when they were wronged (Matt. 5).

Chapter 15: Teachings About Love

Love must be understood in the context of a relationship, so this chapter described the relationships between God, his messenger (Jesus or Muhammad), believers, and unbelievers.

The relationship between God and his messenger set the tone for all the messenger did and taught.

Jesus described a loving relationship between himself and Father God. Consequently, Jesus loved his disciples and urged the disciples to love others, even nonbelievers.

Muhammad spoke of a master-slave relationship with Allah. He didn't speak of loving Allah, and he didn't speak of loving the Muslims. He controlled his followers with rewards and punishments. He told his followers to treat others in the same way—to reward believers with kindness and to punish unbelievers with jihad.

Chapter 16: Teachings on Prayer

In Islam, prayer is a scripted event made up of both words and physical movement. Prayers are required at five specific times each day, and they focus on worshiping Allah and declaring submission to him. Muslims are not forbidden to say additional prayers outside of the script, but they are not encouraged to do so. Personal communication from Allah during prayer is not expected. (Only a small sect called the Sufites hopes for this.) Prayer is a way to earn Allah's favor.

Jesus rejected rote repetition of prayer. For prayer, he taught his disciples to offer worship, ask God to take care of their needs, and ask for forgiveness of sins. Jesus used prayer to communicate with God as a child would to his father. Unlike Muhammad, Jesus told his followers to *pray* for their enemies.

Chapter 17: Attitudes Toward Women

Jesus and Muhammad were very different in their attitudes toward women. We looked at three areas.

Character of women: Muhammad made rather negative comments about women as a group. However, he made sure the material needs of Muslim women in the community were met. Jesus did not make comments about the character of women being different than the character of men. He praised women for their faith, healed those who needed healing, and accepted their assistance.

Teachings about marriage: In marriage Muhammad called for the husband to be the provider and for the wife to be submissive.

208

A husband could divorce his wife for a variety of big and small reasons. The wife could not initiate a divorce or stop a divorce. In contrast, Jesus taught that divorce should only be allowed in the case of adultery. He described marriage as a spiritual union ordained by God.

Marriage in personal life: Muhammad married thirteen women all together and left nine widows. Jesus never married, but he had a group of women who traveled with him to assist him.

CONCLUSION

I hope this review will help you keep the big picture in mind about the relationship between Jesus and Muhammad. Many people look for the similarities between them, but as I looked at their lives side by side, I had to conclude that fundamental differences far outweigh superficial similarities.

More importantly, I realized that I had come to a place where I had to make a personal decision for myself. Which path would I follow? In the next chapter, I will describe my choice.

20

My Personal Decision

My mind had been focused like a laser on the black leather Bible in front of me all night. I had no awareness of time until I heard the sound of a voice over the mosque loudspeaker. It was the call to morning prayer!

I looked in surprise at the clock beside my bed—it was 4 a.m. already. I heard members of my household moving around and getting ready to go to the mosque. But this morning I wasn't even going to pretend to pray. I felt an overwhelming sense of peace, and I just wanted to rest.

After my experience in prison, I struggled with sleep every night. I often spent hours tossing and turning in bed until I would finally fall into an exhausted sleep. But this morning I laid my head on the pillow and within a minute I was sleeping. I didn't even realize that my headache was completely gone.

Three hours later, at 7 a.m., I awoke feeling completely refreshed. I was ready to make my decision. I had found the almighty God of heaven that I had been seeking. With no doubt left in my mind, I prayed to the God of the Bible and pledged my life to him. Then I turned back to the Bible.

I had already finished reading the Gospels, Acts, and Romans. I wasn't sure where to read next, so I just let the pharmacist's Bible fall open. This time I came to Psalm 91. I read the whole psalm. Then I read it again. It sounded like a personal message just for me and my situation.

PSALM 91

He who dwells in the shelter of the Most High
    will rest in the shadow of the Almighty.
I will say of the Lord, "He is my refuge and my fortress,
    my God, in whom I trust."
Surely he will save you from the fowler's snare
    and from the deadly pestilence.
He will cover you with his feathers,
    and under his wings you will find refuge;
    his faithfulness will be your shield and rampart.
You will not fear the terror of night,
    nor the arrow that flies by day,
nor the pestilence that stalks in the darkness,
    nor the plague that destroys at midday.
A thousand may fall at your side,
    ten thousand at your right hand,
    but it will not come near you.
You will only observe with your eyes
    and see the punishment of the wicked.

If you make the Most High your dwelling—
    even the LORD, who is my refuge—
then no harm will befall you,
    no disaster will come near your tent.
For he will command his angels concerning you
    to guard you in all your ways;
they will lift you up in their hands,
    so that you will not strike your foot against a stone.
You will tread upon the lion and the cobra;
    you will trample the great lion and the serpent.

"Because he loves me," says the LORD, "I will rescue him;
    I will protect him, for he acknowledges my name.
He will call upon me, and I will answer him;
    I will be with him in trouble,
    I will deliver him and honor him.
With long life will I satisfy him
    and show him my salvation."

These words told me that God knew the dangers I would face because of my decision. My family, my brothers, my father, my own people—when they learned of my conversion, they would come and try to kill me before anyone else.

In this psalm I heard God say, "I will protect you."

"OK," I decided. "This psalm is the promise of God, and this is the weapon that I am going to carry during my battles." I memorized the entire psalm before I left my room.

TELLING THE PHARMACIST

By 11 a.m. I was back at the pharmacist's shop with my tablets in one hand and the Bible in the other. I went to the counter and gave the tablets back to the pharmacist.

She asked me, "Did you read the Bible?"

I told her, "Yes, and I have decided to become a Christian."

She leaped up and started praising God out loud. Then she ran out from behind the counter and into the shop to give me a hug.

"Come in; sit down," she said motioning me through the little swinging door into the back of the pharmacy. With a big smile on her face, she went off to find a chair for me.

After I was sitting she said, "Wait a minute," and started dialing the phone to make a call. I got very nervous at this point, wondering if she was going to turn me in to the secret police. Maybe this was all a trick.

But she was only calling her husband, a veterinarian who worked for the government. "You've got to come here right away," she said.

When her husband arrived half an hour later, the pharmacist said to me, "We want to hear what happened last night." As I talked, the pharmacist asked questions, but her husband just watched me—silently and intently.

Finally I said, "I want to recite something for you." Then I recited all of Psalm 91. I could see tears in her husband's eyes.

She said, "It's twelve. I am closing the pharmacy, and we are taking you to lunch. After lunch we will take you to our church."

As we ate lunch, they kept me busy with questions about my experience with the Bible the night before. I asked her if she wanted the Bible back. "No," she said. "I want you to keep it."

Then they began to give me some warnings about how I should behave. "Don't tell too many people what you have done," they warned. "Don't walk into a church openly. Too many people will see you. You can come to home Bible studies with us." Even so, they were excited about introducing me to their pastor.

After we talked with the pastor in his office for a while, he reached a conclusion that shocked us all. He basically told me, "My son, you can go back to your home. We do not need to add a number to our congregation. And if you go home, we will not lose any number from our congregation. We are not interested."

He was afraid that radical Muslims would attack his church if they heard that a Muslim apostate was attending services there. As we were leaving his office I told him, "Listen, I am not worried about what you did to me now. The one who saved me will help me and will look after me. Even though you reject me, he will be faithful to me wherever I go. But you need help."

The pharmacist and her husband were so disappointed and embarrassed. They kept apologizing for what happened. I was upset as well, but I could also see that the pastor's attitude did not match what I had just read in the Bible. I was beginning to learn the important principle of separating the leaders from the followers. This is a principle I needed to apply both to Islam and Christianity.

A SECRET CHRISTIAN

For the next year I lived as a "secret Christian" in Egypt. I did not tell my family what I had done, but I casually stopped by the pharmacist's office when I needed to talk. I asked her many questions about the Bible and Christianity. But I never needed to ask her for the headache tablets again. My headaches were gone.

I had a hard time finding a church that would allow me to attend services. I went privately to three different pastors who told me that I was not welcome in their churches. I finally took a taxi to a monastery far in the desert outside of Cairo. It was so remote that I thought they would not be afraid of the secret police in the city. A monk met me outside the walls of the monastery and told me the same story, "We can't help you." But he gave me the name of one more pastor who might help. The next day I went to that church. The pastor was very tough at first, trying to make sure I was honest. He did accept me, and I attended that church cautiously for a year until I left Egypt. I say the word *cautiously*, because I was careful not to draw attention to myself.

I took a bus to church instead of driving my car to avoid being followed by radical Muslims. I did not tell my story to members of the church. Large churches in Egypt usually had an Egyptian policeman serving as a security guard at the door of the church. Until the policeman got used to seeing me, I concealed myself within in a large group of people when I went in and out of the door. I had to make sure he did not stop me and find out who I was.

During the day, I continued to work with my father as a sales director for his clothing factory.

Leaving Egypt

It was only a matter of time before my family found out. One day, completely unplanned, I blurted out the truth to my father. Immediately my father pulled his handgun out of his shoulder holster and fired five bullets at me. Within days I left my home and Egypt permanently. This was the beginning of a long journey that took me from Egypt to South Africa and, finally, to the United States, where this book was written.

I carried the pharmacist's Bible with me, and I have it to this day. She paid a price for helping me. After I left Egypt, radical Muslims burned down her pharmacy, trying to kill her. Coptic Christians in Egypt told me that she and her husband left the country and immigrated to Canada.

MY LIFE TODAY

I have lived as a Christian for the past eleven years, devoting myself to giving Muslims and all people the opportunity to learn about Jesus just as I did.

No one should be forced to accept any belief system. But everyone should have access to any information they want and the opportunity to make a decision without the fear of what other people might do to them.

I pray that my words have supplied you with the light that will lead you toward peace, joy, and forgiveness from the almighty God.

Epilogue

If someone tells you a story and you want to find out whether it is true, what do you do? You go back to the original source.

This has been the intention of this book: to help you understand Islam and Christianity by taking you to their founders. Remember: you cannot understand Christianity by what Christians do, nor can you understand Islam by what Muslims do. You have to go to the original sources.

This book is unique in several ways:

- There are only a handful of English-language books in print that focus on the comparison between Jesus and Muhammad.

- Few English-language books about Islam are based on a thorough knowledge of the Quran, hadith, and Islamic history studied in the original Arabic.

- Many English-language books about Islam look for common ground between Islam and Christianity. This book lets the differences between Jesus and Muhammad speak for themselves.

Every reader will react differently to this book:

- Some will complain that I am trying to make Muslims look bad. This is not my intention. I know that most Muslims are wonderful, kind, generous people who want to live at peace with the world. I came out of the Muslim culture, and I still love the Muslim people.

- Some will be offended at the idea of challenging Muhammad in any way. This is the mindset of the conservative Muslim community where I grew up. I hope they will be able to move past this attitude and look at the information with an open mind.

· Some will be skeptical, wondering if I have withheld information or presented a warped picture. I encourage these people to check the original sources for themselves.

· Some Christians will decide to change their belief that Christianity and Islam are based on the same God. I hope they will let other Christians know about what they have learned. I pray this will motivate Christians to work harder to share the gospel with Muslims.

· Some people will be attracted to Jesus and his message. This is the best possible outcome of reading this book.

I cannot know what your personal reaction will be, but if you see the truth in Jesus, I encourage you to read the Bible and talk with sincere Christians about this wonderful way of life. "You will know the truth, and the truth will set you free" (John 8:32).

Jesus declared:

> I am the way and the truth and the life. No one comes
> to the Father except through me.
>
> —JOHN 14:6

Jesus offers a kind of love that no other prophet in history ever offered:

> Come to me, all you who are weary and burdened,
> and I will give you rest. Take my yoke upon you and
> learn from me, for I am gentle and humble in heart,
> and you will find rest for your souls. For my yoke is
> easy and my burden is light.
>
> —MATTHEW 11:28–30

I pray you will come to rest in his love.

Appendix A

The Sources of Information About Jesus and Muhammad

Have you ever been talking with a friend who starts to tell you something and you have no idea what he is talking about? You understand the words he is using, but he has forgotten to tell you the topic of his conversation.

Many western readers who try to read the Quran or hadith feel the same way. They can read the English translations, but they need more information in order for the words to make sense.

Throughout this book I rely heavily on quotes from the Quran, hadith, and the Gospels to explain the stories of Jesus and Muhammad. This appendix will give you the historical keys to interpreting the Quran and other Islamic writings.

It will also address a fundamental issue for Muslims and Christians alike—the reliability of the Gospels. Muslims believe that Christians and Jews have corrupted their Scriptures by changing some words or removing some parts (Surah 5:12–15). We will look to see whether there is evidence to support this claim.

This appendix is one of the most important chapters in this book. Not only will it help you understand what you are reading in this book, but it will also help you interpret what other people are saying about Islam and Christianity.

SOURCES OF INFORMATION ABOUT MUHAMMAD

Information about Muhammad comes from four primary sources:

1. The Quran
2. The hadith
3. Biographies of Muhammad
4. Islamic history

Let's look at the keys to understanding each source.

THE QURAN

The Islamic faith is based upon the Quran, which is a book that is a little shorter than the Christian New Testament. Muhammad dictated the Quran to his followers based on the revelations that he said he received from the angel Gabriel. Muhammad said Gabriel brought these revelations directly from Allah.

So the language of the Quran is based on the idea of Allah speaking to Muhammad. That's why many verses begin with the phrase, "Say, O Muhammad…" The format of the Quran is Allah telling Muhammad what to say. Many verses will also start with the word *Remember*. Again, this format is Allah telling Muhammad to remember something.

Whenever you see a first-person reference in the Quran, it refers to Allah. Sometimes you will see the word *We*. This is also a reference to Allah. The plurality is used to show the greatness of Allah, not to teach that there is more than one almighty God.

Regarding information about Muhammad, the Quran is our most reliable source because Muhammad was in complete control of what was recorded as a Quranic revelation. He was the only one who could declare that a word came from Allah and needed to be collected for the Quran.

Muhammad reported revelations from the angel Gabriel for a period of twenty-three years. Many of these revelations were responses to historical events, such as a battle or a question about behavior in Islamic society. The Quran can be confusing unless you are aware of these corresponding events. Some copies of the Quran will give you information about the context of certain passages. Muslims also rely on Quranic commentaries to guide them on this issue.

One commentary in English that is easy to access is *The Meaning of the Quran* by Syed Maududi.

In this book I supply you with the pertinent historical background for the quotes I use from the Quran.

The question of language

Traditional Muslims believe the Quran can only be understood in its original language—classical Arabic. When I was a child, my uncle took great effort to train me in the classical Arabic. Without special training, Arabic speakers cannot understand classical Arabic, which is used not only in the Quran, but also in the hadith and other early literature. To understand these texts, most Muslims rely on commentaries and what they are taught at the mosque or through Muslim media.

Muslims who can read the classical Arabic are very hesitant to translate the texts into English because Islamic tradition says that classical Arabic is the language of heaven. Therefore, the English translations of the Quran and hadith are almost always made by people who are not native Arabic speakers. Their translations convey the idea of the text, but at times their understanding of the Arabic is not clear, and, as a result, their choice of English words is sometimes unclear as well.

When I do my research, I read the sources in the original Arabic. After finding the information in my Arabic-language books, I cross-reference it to the English translations. Most of the time these translations are adequate, but occasionally I will use my own translation for clarity. Information about both Arabic and English references are included in the notes and bibliography.

HADITH

Many well-educated westerners do not have an understanding of the second most important body of literature in Islamic theology—the hadith.

Rather than give you an academic definition of hadith, I will start by telling you how they were created.

Let me give you a picture from the life of Muhammad. He is at his house in Medina with one of his servants (Abu Haraira) when a man is brought before him who has drunk wine in violation of Islamic law. Muhammad commands the Muslims to beat him as punishment. The servant observes all of this and commits the story to memory. The next time a similar situation occurs, the servant tells people, "I heard the prophet say such and such in this situation."[1]

After Muhammad's death, information about his life and teachings became very precious. The servant began to worry that if he got sick and died that the story would be lost. So he asked someone who was literate to write it down on a scroll. This scroll would be precious and carefully passed down from generation to generation.

This story is an example of a hadith. The word *hadith* means "an account of something that Muhammad did or taught." You may speak of one hadith or collections of hadith.

The servant in the previous story is an example of a narrator of hadith. Almost every hadith will present its narrator, the one who is credited with first telling the story. This servant is credited for the narration of thousands of hadith. Muhammad's other servants, his closest companions, and his wives (especially Aisha) are also credited with hadith. When I list the sources for hadith, I sometimes include the name of the narrator because it supplies good information about the reliability of the hadith.

Let's see how the hadith were collected and preserved to the present day. Two hundred years after Muhammad's death, a rich tradition of scholarship had developed in the Islamic community. Scholars in different areas were studying the hadith that were available to them. These religious teachers began to see the need to collect the hadith from different places and to put them all together. So they traveled and talked to all the families and people who had descended from those who had direct contact with Muhammad. These people reported the hadith that they had saved on scrolls or passed down in oral history. The two most respected editors of hadith are Al-Bukhari (A.H. 194–256) and Muslim (A.H. 202–261), who were collecting hadith during the same time period.

Al-Bukhari and Muslim did not accept every story that people told them about Muhammad. They first looked for the original source of the story, or the narrator, to see if this person would be a reliable source for the information in the hadith. They also compared the story to other accounts about Muhammad to see if they were consistent. Only then was the hadith added to the collection.

Bukhari chose 9,082 hadith for his collection. However, this number reflected multiple retellings of the same story. When these repetitions are accounted for, there are about 2,602 separate accounts regarding Muhammad's life. Muslim's collection contains a total of approximately 4,000 hadith, including the repetition.[2]

Are there any inaccurate stories in the hadith? Yes, of course. Even Muslim scholars recognize that this process could not be perfect. Hundreds of years ago scholars began to evaluate the reliability of the different collections of hadith. Out of these, the scholars chose six collections that are considered most reliable and are known as the "correct books" of the hadith (*sahih*). The most respected is *Sahih al-Bukhari* followed by *Sahih Muslim*.

In modern times even the correct books of hadith have been put under scrutiny. There is a complex "science of hadith" that evaluates each story on the basis of its reliability. The most famous Muslim scholar in the science of hadith is al-Elbani, who has divided the hadith from all six of the correct books of hadith into two sets—one labeled weak and the other labeled correct.

For a westerner, this sounds like an academic debate, but if you work in the Middle East as an imam or lecturer, this is information you need on a daily basis. As an imam, I remember a man who saw me washing before prayer and challenged the way I was cleansing my hair. "Why do you wash like that?" he asked. "It says in the hadith of Muwatta to do it a different way."

I answered him, "Yes, I know what Muwatta says, but Bukhari says it this way, and Bukhari is more correct than Muwatta."

What is the difference between hadith and the Quran?

For the purpose of gaining information about Muhammad, there is a key difference that needs to be recognized regarding the Quran and hadith. Muhammad was completely involved in what was added to the collection of Quranic revelations. In contrast, Muhammad did not have direct control over what was preserved as hadith. Sometimes people just watched him and reported what they saw. Sometimes Muhammad told people stories, and they repeated them. But he could not control the information they repeated or its accuracy.

This difference becomes pertinent when you consider an issue such as miracles. The Quran says that Muhammad was just a man who would *not* do signs to prove that he was a prophet of Allah. However, the hadith contain various stories about Muhammad performing miracles. (See chapter 12, "Healings and Miracles.") How do we handle this contradiction? Since the Quran came directly through the mouth of Muhammad, we have to consider Quranic information most reliable as an indication of what Muhammad actually did. Therefore, Islamic scholars tend to say that many of the miracle stories in the hadith were invented by Muhammad's followers.

OTHER SOURCES OF INFORMATION ABOUT MUHAMMAD

In addition to the hadith, Islamic scholars also rely on two other types of books—biographies of Muhammad and Islamic histories. I have used the following two sources in the book you are reading.

The most popular and trusted biography of Muhammad was written by Ibn Ishaq (A.H. 83–132). His writing predates Bukhari and Muslim by about seventy years, but it is considered a little less reliable. However, he would have based his biography on the same hadith that Bukhari and Muslim collected seventy years later. Ibn Ishaq's work was edited and popularized about seventy years later by Ibn Hisham. My Arabic copy of it is published in three volumes with a total of 1,020 pages. Ironically, Ibn Ishaq's grandfather was a Christian from Iraq who was forcibly converted to Islam by the first caliph after Muhammad's death.[3]

I have also used information from one of the most thorough Islamic history books, *The Beginning and the End* written by Ibn Kathir (A.H. 700–774). Ibn Kathir produced a massive work that described the history of the world from the Islamic point of view, starting with creation and ending just before the author's death in A.H. 774. I have read through this work more than once because it is a book we studied in detail at Al-Azhar. This nine-volume set is not available in English.

Although these books do not have the same reverence as the correct books of hadith, they are useful in supplying information about Muhammad.

Now let's consider a major challenge that Muslims present regarding the Bible.

WAS THE BIBLE CORRUPTED?

Muhammad taught that Christians and Jews corrupted the Bible. In other words, he said that the Bible was accurate when it was first recorded but Jews and Christians later changed it to suit their own goals.

Regarding the Jews, the Quran says:

> [The children of Israel] changed the words from their (right) places and have abandoned a good part of the Message that was sent to them.
>
> —SURAH 5:13

Regarding Christians, the Quran says:

> And from those who call themselves Christians...they
> have abandoned a good part of the Message that was
> sent to them.
> —SURAH 5:14; SEE ALSO VERSE 15

Muhammad claimed that if the Scriptures had not been corrupted, then they would still contain the prophecies regarding his coming.

Did Muhammad explain when or how the Scriptures were corrupted or who did it? No. Did he offer any proof of these changes by presenting an unchanged copy of the Scriptures? No.

Archeological finds in the past century, however, refute Muhammad's teaching. There are two popular Christian books available right now that describe how the New Testament has been preserved accurately. These are *The Case for Christ* by Lee Strobel (HarperCollins/Zondervan), especially chapter 3, and *Jesus: The Great Debate* by Grant R. Jeffrey (Word). Let's look at their evidence regarding the reliability of the Gospels.

If you are researching the reliability of an ancient document, you will look for three things:

1. The amount of time passing between the original and the oldest known copy

2. The number of copies found from ancient sources

3. The consistency between ancient copies and modern copies

Point #1: age of oldest manuscripts

The historical evidence for reliability of the New Testament dwarfs the amount of evidence for the reliability of any other ancient manuscript.

The oldest discovered fragment of the New Testament was five verses from the Book of John found on a fragment of papyrus from Egypt. Based on the style of the script, the fragment was dated between A.D. 100 and 150. This is only fifteen to sixty-five years after the time when the Book of John was believed to have been written.

This is powerful evidence, especially compared to the evidence available regarding other manuscripts from this time. For example, the oldest fragment of the historical record of Tacitus, written in about A.D. 116, is dated A.D. 850.

The most significant discovery of New Testament texts are papyri dating from about the A.D. 300, which contain portions of the four Gospels and the Book of Acts, and papyri dating from about A.D. 200, which contain portions of the Epistles and the Book of Hebrews.

Another important discovery was a complete copy of the New Testament (*Codex Sinaiticus*) dated at A.D. 350.

Point #2: quantity of manuscripts

In all there are total of 5,644 manuscripts recording portions of the New Testament in Greek, its original language. An additional 19,000 copies are available in other languages such as Latin, Ethiopic, Slavic, and Armenian.

Compared to the number of copies available of other ancient manuscripts, this figure is enormous. Next to the New Testament, the manuscript with the greatest number of corroborating copies is Homer's *Iliad*, which has only 650 Greek manuscripts surviving today.

Point #3: consistency of manuscripts

Were there discrepancies among the various manuscripts of the New Testament? Other than minor copying errors, the answer is no. Not one Christian doctrine is affected by these minor differences.[4]

This evidence gives strong proof that the New Testament in use during the time of Muhammad and the New Testament used today are faithful copies of the original books. Now that we have established the reliability of the copies of the New Testament, let's look at how the Gospels were written.

Appendix A

SOURCES OF INFORMATION ABOUT JESUS

For information about Jesus I relied upon the four Gospels recorded in the New Testament: Matthew, Mark, Luke, and John. Similar to hadith, these are accounts of what Jesus did and taught as recorded by his followers.

New evidence shows that these Gospels were written within less than sixty years after the death of Jesus by authors who were either eyewitnesses of what occurred or people who were in contact with eyewitnesses.

Here are brief biographies of each Gospel writer.[5]

Biography of Matthew

Before Jesus called him to be one of his twelve disciples, Matthew was a tax collector. As a Jew, Matthew wrote this book especially for the Jewish people, often quoting Old Testament prophecies in reference to Jesus. He wrote this book between A.D. 60 and 65, which would have been about thirty years after the death of Jesus. We can guess that Matthew was about the same age as Jesus when he became a disciple, which means he was probably in his sixties when he was writing this book. Church history suggests that he lived to the age of ninety, and died either of natural causes or by the sword.

Biography of Mark

Mark was not one of the twelve disciples, but it is believed that he was one of the seventy disciples that Jesus sent out to preach and show signs to the people. He is mentioned in the Book of Acts as John Mark. His presentation of Jesus' life shows the personality of Jesus through his miracles and teaching. When Mark was spending time with the believers in Rome between A.D. 55 and 65, he wrote his book. It is considered to be the first Gospel written. Mark was martyred in Alexandria. He was tied to a horse by a rope and dragged through the streets until he died.

Biography of Luke

Luke is a unique writer of the Gospels in several ways. He was a Greek medical doctor, the only Gentile to write a Gospel. He was also the only author who did not personally travel with Jesus. He was a partner with the apostle Paul on most of his mission trips, and he learned the story of Jesus through Paul and his contacts with other Christians. Luke wrote with the gentile reader in mind. His purpose was to give a detailed description of the life of Jesus and to present Jesus as the perfect man and savior. Biblical scholars believe he wrote this book around A.D. 60 either in Rome or Caesarea.

Biography of John

John was a very old man when he wrote this book—probably in his eighties. Written after the destruction of Jerusalem, some time between A.D. 85 and 90, this was the last of the biblical gospels to be recorded. John wrote from a theological point of view: his purpose was to declare that Jesus Christ is the son of God who offers eternal life to those who believe. After he wrote this gospel, John was sent to starve to death on the island of Patmos but was later released and died a natural death.

DIFFERENCES BETWEEN THE GOSPELS AND HADITH

You have probably noticed that there are many circumstantial differences between the hadith and the Gospels. Let's look at these differences and see if they affect our study of Jesus and Muhammad.

The first major difference is when the books were established. The hadith were not formally collected until two hundred years after Muhammad's death while three out of the four Gospels were written by people who personally walked with Jesus. Even though the hadith have more opportunity for error to be introduced, I believe the overall picture of Muhammad is still accurate.

A second difference is in the organization of material. The hadith are not presented in the order of occurrence in

Muhammad's life. You must look for bits and pieces of information in order to complete the big picture. Because of the format of the hadith, it is difficult for a person without special education to fully understand them. In contrast, the Gospels begin with Jesus' birth and walk through his life to his death and resurrection. They are easy to understand without additional information.

Third, the quantity of information is not equal. There are approximately half a million hadith compared to the total of ninety chapters in the Gospels. However, even though the Gospel record is short, it still presents a complete picture of Jesus' life.

In conclusion, even though there are circumstantial differences between hadith and the Gospels, I believe they both provide accurate information.

CONCLUSION

You are now prepared to have a good understanding of the quotes that you read in this book from our five key sources about the lives of Jesus and Muhammad:

- The Quran
- The hadith
- Biographies of Muhammad
- Islamic histories
- The Gospels

Appendix B

Islamic Teaching Regarding Biblical Prophecies About Muhammad

Did you know that according to the Quran, the coming of Muhammad was prophesied in the Bible?

> And verily, it (the Quran, and its revelation to Prophet Muhammad), is (announced) in the Scriptures [i.e. the Taurat (Torah) and the Injeel (Gospel) of former people.
>
> —SURAH 26:196

So why don't we see these prophecies clearly? The Quran teaches that Jews and Christians changed almost all the parts of their Scriptures that spoke about Muhammad.

> They change the words from their (right) places and have abandoned a good part of the Message that was sent to them.
>
> —SURAH 5:13

However, Muslim scholars say, "There exists in the *Taurat* (Torah) and the *Injeel* (Gospel), even after the original text has been distorted, clear prophecies indicating the coming of the Prophet Muhammad."[1]

Let's look now at the Bible verses cited by these Muslim scholars. We will go chronologically through the Bible.

THE PROPHET

In the following passage God is speaking to Moses:

> I will raise up for them a prophet like you from among
> their brothers; I will put my words in his mouth, and
> he will tell them everything I command him.
>
> —DEUTERONOMY 18:18

God was telling Moses that he would give the children of Israel a prophet so that the people would not have to hear his voice directly. This was fulfilled in the history of the children of Israel, for they received many prophets.

THE CORNERSTONE

> The stone the builders rejected has become the
> capstone; the LORD has done this, and it is marvelous
> in our eyes.
>
> —PSALM 118:22–23

Jesus quoted this prophecy in Matthew 21:42–43, indicating that he was the fulfillment.

THE COMING LIGHT

> Here is my servant, whom I uphold, my chosen one in
> whom I delight; I will put my Spirit on him and he will
> bring justice to the nations. He will not shout or cry out,
> or raise his voice in the streets....I, the LORD, have called
> you in righteousness; I will take hold of your hand. I will
> keep you and will make you to be a covenant for the
> people and a light for the Gentiles, to open eyes that are
> blind, and to free captives from prison and to release
> from the dungeon those who sit in darkness.
>
> —ISAIAH 42:1–2, 6–7

Again, Christians believe strongly that this prophecy refers to Jesus, who lived six hundred years before Muhammad.

HOLY ONE FROM MOUNT PARAN

> God came from Teman, the Holy One from Mount
> Paran. His glory covered the heavens and his praise
> filled the earth.
>
> —HABAKKUK 3:3

The part of this verse that Muslims focus on is "the Holy One from Mount Paran." Muslims say Mount Paran is at Mecca, which was the birthplace of Muhammad. But in reality, Mount Paran is not in Arabia; it is in the Sinai Desert. So this prophecy does *not* make reference to Muhammad's birthplace.

THE COUNSELOR

> And I will ask the Father, and he will give you another
> Counselor to be with you forever—the Spirit of truth.
> The world cannot accept him, because it neither sees
> him nor knows him. But you know him, for he lives
> with you and will be in you.
>
> —JOHN 14:16–17

Christians agree that this is a reference to the Holy Spirit living inside a Christian believer. In addition, this verse says several things that are not true about Muhammad. For example, it says the counselor would be with them "forever." Muhammad did not stay with his followers forever. He died. It also says that the world could neither see or know him. But Muhammad was seen and known by many people. Finally, it says that the Counselor would live inside the people. Muhammad could not live inside anybody, because he was not a spirit.

> But the Counselor, the Holy Spirit, whom the Father
> will send in my name, will teach you all things and will
> remind you of everything I have said to you.
>
> —JOHN 14:26

This verse clearly says that the Counselor is the Holy Spirit.

> But I tell you the truth: It is for your good that I am
> going away. Unless I go away, the Counselor will not
> come to you.
>
> —JOHN 16:7

Again, Jesus' prophecy of the Holy Spirit as the coming Comforter is taken to refer to Muhammad.

Remember, Jesus later said more about this prophecy. When he was being taken up to heaven, he said, "Do not leave Jerusalem, but wait for the gift my Father promised, which you have heard me speak about. For John baptized with water, but in a few days you will be baptized with the Holy Spirit" (Acts 1:4–5). Later that promise was fulfilled on the Day of Pentecost when they heard the sound of a violent wind, saw tongues of fire, and were filled with the Holy Spirit (Acts 2:1–4).

CONCLUSION

As you can see for yourself, these prophecies had their fulfillment outside of Muhammad. This is another indication of the weakness of Islamic doctrine about the corruption of Scriptures.

Appendix C

Old Testament Prophecies About Jesus

One of the important proofs that Jesus told the truth is the many Old Testament prophecies that were fulfilled through his life. Below is a list of some of these prophecies with references from the Old Testament and the New Testament.

1. JESUS CHRIST IS THE SEED OF ABRAHAM.

Old Testament
Genesis 22:18
Genesis 49:10
Isaiah 11:1

New Testament
Matthew 1:1–16

2. JESUS IS FROM THE HOUSE OF JESSE.

Old Testament
Isaiah 11:1,10

New Testament
Matthew 1:5–16

3. JESUS CHRIST IS BORN IN BETHLEHEM.

Old Testament
Micah 5:2

New Testament
Matthew 2:1

4. JESUS CHRIST IS BORN FROM A VIRGIN.

Old Testament	*New Testament*
Isaiah 7:14	Luke 1:26–33

5. JESUS CHRIST WAS CALLED FROM EGYPT.

Old Testament	*New Testament*
Hosea 11:1	Matthew 2:14–15

6. JESUS' MINISTRY, HUMILITY, AND MIRACLES.

Old Testament	*New Testament*
Isaiah 35:4–6	Matthew 11:28–30
Isaiah 42:1–4	Matthew 11:2–5

7. JESUS IS THE SAVIOR OF THE WORLD.

Old Testament	*New Testament*
Genesis 3:15	Matthew 18:11
	Luke 19:10
	John 12:47

8. JESUS ENTERS JERUSALEM RIDING A MULE.

Old Testament	*New Testament*
Zechariah 9:9	Matthew 21:7–11

9. JESUS CHRIST WAS BETRAYED.

Old Testament	*New Testament*
Zechariah 11:12–13	Matthew 27:3–8

10. Jesus left alone and the fleeing of the disciples.

Old Testament
Isaiah 53:1–3

New Testament
Matthew 26:56

11. Jesus remains silent during his trial and dies for the world's salvation.

Old Testament
Isaiah 53:4–8

New Testament
Matthew 26:63
Matthew 27:14
John 18:14

12. Jesus during the events of the Crucifixion.

Old Testament
Isaiah 50:6
Psalm 22:1–18
Psalm 69:21

New Testament
Matthew 26:67
Matthew 27:26, 35, 39,
43, 46, 48

13. Jesus is crucified between two thieves and buried in a rich man's tomb.

Old Testament
Isaiah 53:9

New Testament
Matthew 27:38, 57–60

14. Jesus rises from the dead and frees the souls of those who died in hope of resurrection.

Old Testament
Psalm 16:10
Psalm 24:7–10

New Testament
Matthew 28:5–7
1 Peter 3:19

Appendix D

Jesus in the Quran and the Bible

This chart focuses specifically on teachings in the Quran about Jesus that are confirmed in the Bible. Therefore it does not include teachings from the Quran that disagree with the Bible. This chart will give you a wealth of information toward understanding the mindset of Muslims toward Jesus.

TITLES	QURAN	BIBLE
A Man of Peace (*Salam*)	19:33–34	Isa. 9:6; Dan. 19:25
A Perfect Man (*Sawiyan*)	19:17	1 Cor. 13:10
Apostle (Messenger) (*Rasul*)	2:81–87, 253–254; 3:43–49	Heb. 3:1; Matt. 10:40
A Spirit from God (*Ruh*)	4:169–171	Matt. 12:28; Luke 1:35
A Word from God. His (God's) Word (*Kalimah*)	3:34–39, 40–45; 4:169–171	John 1:1, 14
A Word of Truth (*qawl Al-haqq*)	19:35–34	John 14:6; Eph. 1:13
An Example (pattern) (*Mathal*)	43:57–59	John 13:1–11
Bearer of Wisdom (*Hikmah*)	43:63	Luke 2:40–52
The Chaste (*Hasuwur*)	3:39	2 Cor. 5:21; 1 Pet. 2:21

Highly Honored (Eminent) in this World and Hereafter (*Wajihan*)	3:40–45	Phil. 2:2–10
Giver of Good Tidings	61:6	Luke 4:18; Acts 10:38
Knowledge of the Hour (*Ilm*)	43:61	Matt. 24:36–44; John 4:25
Knowledgeable in Scriptures	3:43–48; 5:109–110	Matthew 12:25; John 4:25
Like of Adam (*Mathal Adam*)	3:52–59	1 Cor. 15:45–47
Messiah (*Al-Masih*)	3:40–45; 4:156–157	Matt. 16:16; John 1:41
Mercy from Us (Good)	19:21	Matt. 9:27–30
Miracle Worker	3:49	Mark 1:34; 5:41–42; 6:33
Noble (Lordly) (*Sayyid*)	3:39	Matthew 21: 8–10
One of the Righteous (*min al Salihin*)	3:40–46	Matt. 27:19; 2 Tim. 4
One of the Closest to God	3:40–41; 7:111–114	John 14:9–10; Heb. 2
Prophet (*Nabiyy*)	2:130–136; 4:161–163	Matt. 21:11; Luke 4:24
Revelation to Mankind (*Ayah*)	19:21	Luke 2:10, 30–32
Servant of God (*Abd Allah*)	4:170–172; 19:31	Matt. 12:18; John 4:34
Sign to All Beings (*Ayah*)	3:44–50; 19:21; 21:91	Matt. 2:2–9
Sign of the Hour (Judgment Day)	23:50	Matt. 24:37–38; Acts 1:11
Son of Mary (*Ibn Maryam*)	3:40–45; 4:157–171	Luke 2:48
The Blessed One (*Mubarak*)	19:31–32	Matthew 21:9; Luke 1:42

The Faultless Son (Holy, Most Pure) (*Zakiyyn*)	19:19	Luke 23:4, 14, 41; Acts 2:14
The One Confirmed (Strengthened with the Holy Spirit) (*Ruh Al-Quds*)	2:81–87, 253–254	Mark 1:11; Luke 4:14
The One to Be Followed	43:61	John 1:37; 10:27
The One to Be Obeyed	3:44–50	Matt. 8:27; 17:5; Mark 1:3
The Truth From Your Lord (*All-haqq*)	3:53–60	John 8:32–36; 14:6
Witness on Resurrection Day (*Shahid*)	4:45; 5:117	Matt. 24
Witness Over the People	5:120–117	John 5:30

Notes

Editor's note: Unless otherwise noted, translations of Arabic materials are by the author.

CHAPTER 1
GROWING UP IN ISLAM

1. Islam for Today, s.v. Al-Azhar University, Cairo, "Historical Background," http://www.islamfortoday.com/alazhar.htm, (accessed December 17, 2003).

CHAPTER 4
CHILDHOOD DESTINIES

1. Ibn Hisham, *The Life of Muhammad*, 3rd ed., vol. 1, pt. 1 (Beirut, Lebanon: Dar-al-Jil, 1998), p. 295. Narrated Othman Ibn Abi El-Aas. Also see Ibn Kathir, *The Beginning and the End*, vol. 1, pt. 2 (Beruit, Lebanon: The Revival of the Arabic Tradition Publishing House, 2001), p. 289. I have mentioned this anecdote about Muhammad's mother because it is familiar to most Muslims; however, there is some question as to whether it is authentic. Muhammad himself never told this story. It was thirty years after Muhammad's death that Othman reported receiving this story from his mother. So this raises the possibility that Othman introduced the story to help convince people that Muhammad was a true prophet. Othman's comment about stars may have been inspired by the Quran's retelling of the story of Joseph where Joseph told his father that he saw the sun, moon, and stars bowing before him (Surah 12).

2. *Sahih Muslim* (*The Correct Books of Muslim*), English translation by Abdul Hamid Siddiqui. (New Delhi, India: Kitab Bhaven, 2000; Chicago, IL: Kazi Publications 1976), bk. 1, no. 311. Material was accessed at the University of Southern California website, 2003. Narrated by Anas ibn Malik. Other hadith also record this story with the most popular versions describing two angels at the scene.

3. Dr. A. Shalaby, *Encyclopedia of Islamic History* (Cairo, Egypt: *Dar al-Nahadah*, 1973).

4. Ibn Kathir, *The Beginning and the End*, vol. 1, pt. 2, p. 297. Also see Ibn Hisham, vol. 1, pt. 1, p. 321, and Ibn Ishaq, *The Life of Muhammad: A Translation of Ibn Ishaq's Sirat Rasul Allah*, translated by A. Guillaume, 16th printing (Karachi, Pakistan: Oxford University Press, 2003), pp. 79–81.

CHAPTER 5
THE BEGINNING OF THE REVELATIONS

1. Ibn Ishaq, p. 82.

2. Abu Musa al-Hariri, *Priest and Prophet: Research on the Rise of Islam*, 13th ed. (Lebanon: House for the Advancement of Scholarship, 1991), 231 p. 37. Al-Hariri listed several sources for his information about Waraqa, including: *Tabakat ibn Saad*, vol. 1, pp. 19, 129, 131, 156, 168; *As Sirah al Halabiyah*, vol. 1, pp. 147, 152–153; *Al Sirah Al Mecciyah*, vol. 1, p. 188; *The History of the Prophet and the Kings*, known as *Tarif Al-Tabari*, vol. 2, p. 281; Ibn Hisham, vol. 1, p. 174. I discovered this book after I became a Christian and was living in South Africa. Abu Musa is a pen name for a Marionite monk from Lebanon who writes about the relationship between Islam and Christianity. This monk spent his life in a monastery, researching the relationship between the Bible and the Quran, and between Christianity and the revelation of Muhammad. The book is well known in Arabic-speaking Christian circles in the Middle East. What shocked me was that this monk was writing powerfully in the classical Arabic. I didn't think any Christian had the ability to use this language. This monk very skillfully used the Quran, hadith, and other historical sources. For example, I knew about Waraqa from my studies at Al-Azhar, but I did not know much about the beliefs of his sect, the Ebionites. At Al-Azhar, we were never given any information or sign that Muhammad was influenced by outside sources. This book was given to me by a missionary from Lebanon who took classes from the author at a Catholic seminary in Lebanon. Whenever the monk cited information from the Quran or hadith, I double-checked him, and he was correct. I could not check some of his sources just because the books were not available to me. This book has not been translated into English yet.

3. Jesus-Institute.org, History and Timeline of Jesus, "First Century Context of Palestine (Israel)," educational setting, www.jesus-institute.org (accessed January 2, 2004).

4. *Sahih al-Bukhari (The Correct Books of Bukhari)*, vol. 9, bk. 93, no. 588, English translation by Dr. Muhammad Muhasin Khan. Material was accessed at the University of Southern California website, 2003.

5. Al Hariri, *Priest and Prophet*.

6. *The Correct Books of Bukhari*, vol. 6, bk. 60, no. 478 and vol. 4, bk, 55, no. 605. This hadith is also recorded with a slight variation, saying that Waraqa wrote in Hebrew rather than Arabic. (See *The Correct Books of Bukhari*, vol. 1, bk. 1, no. 3.)

7. Ibn Kathir, *The Beginning and the End*.

8. This story was reported by Aisha, the second wife of Muhammad, who said she heard it from Muhammad herself. Both *The Correct Books of Muslim* and *The Correct Books of Bukhari* report the story in their collections with only minor differences between them. See *The Correct Books of Bukhari*, vol. 9, bk. 87, no. 111 and vol. 1, bk. 1, no. 3; *The Correct Books of Muslim*, bk. 1, no. 301.

9. This aspect of the story was narrated by Abdullah bin al Zubair, the son of one of Muhammad's closest friends. It is recorded in Ibn Hisham, vol. 1, pt. 2, p. 73.

10. Ibn Hisham, vol. 1, pt. 2, p. 73.

11. *The Correct Books of Bukhari*, vol. 1, bk. 1, no. 3, and vol. 6, bk. 60, no. 478.

12. Ibid., vol. 9, bk. 87, no. 111. Narrated by Aisha.

13. *The Correct Books of Muslim*, bk. 1, no. 307. Narrated by Jabir.

14. *The Correct Books of Bukhari*, vol. 1, bk. 1, no. 3.

CHAPTER 6
THE PEOPLE RESPOND

1. Ibn Ishaq, pp. 111, 114.

2. Ibn Hisham, vol. 1, pt. 2, p. 91.

3. Ibn Ishaq, p. 115.

4. Ibid., p. 112.

5. Ibid., p. 118.

6. Ibid., p. 119.

7. Ibid., p. 131.

8. Ibid., p. 145.

9. Ibn Hisham, vol. 1, part 2, p. 222ff. Ibn Ishaq, *The Life of Muhammad*, p. 159ff.

10. Ibn Ishaq, p. 160.

11. Ibid., p. 191.

12. Ibid., pp. 194–195.

13. Ibid., p. 194.

14. Ibid., p. 203. In Islamic history, this event is referred to as the "second pledge of al-Aqaba."

15. Ibid., p. 204.

CHAPTER 7
SPREADING THE MESSAGE

1. Ibn Kathir, *The Beginning and the End*, vol. 2, pt. 3, p. 215.

2. Ibn Ishaq, p. 324ff.

3. Ibid., p. 280.

4. Ibid., pp. 281–286.

5. Ibid., p. 297.

6. Ibid., pp. 659–660.

7. Ibid., p. 368.

8. *The Correct Books of Bukhari*, vol. 5, bk. 59, no. 447.

9. *The Correct Books of Muslim*, bk. 19, no. 4347.

10. *The Correct Books of Bukhari*, vol. 7, bk. 62, no. 88. Narrated by Ursa.

CHAPTER 8
LAST DAYS

1. Ibn Ishaq, p. 557.
2. Ibn Kathir, *The Beginning and the End*, vol. 2, pt. 3, p. 53.
3. Ibn Ishaq, p. 548.
4. Ibn Kathir, *The Beginning and the End*, vol. 2, pt. 4, p. 302.
5. Ibid., vol. 2, pt. 4, p. 289.
6. Ibid., vol. 2, pt. 3, p. 288.
7. *The Correct Books of Muslim*, bk. 19, no. 4395.
8. Ibn Ishaq, pp. 627–652. See also *Al-Tijab al-Najar* (*The Biography of the Prophet*) in Arabic (Cairo, 1979).
9. Ibn Hisham, vol. 3, pt. 6, pp. 13–14. See also Ibn Ishaq, *The Life of Muhammad*, p. 652ff
10. Ibn Hisham, vol. 3, pt. 6, pp. 13–14; author's translation. See also *The Correct Books of Muslim*, bk. 019, no. 4380. The narration in Muslim is slightly different from the narration in Ibn Hisham.
11. *The Correct Books of Muslim*, bk. 7, no. 2802.
12. Ibn Hisham, pt. 6, vol. 3, p. 8; author's translation.
13. Ibn Ishaq, p. 516. See also Ibn Hisham, vol. 2, pt. 4, p. 309.
14. Ibn Ishaq, p. 679ff.

CHAPTER 9
TIME LINES

1. The dates for this timeline were derived from the *Life Application Bible* (Netherlands: Tyndale House Publishers, 1999). The exact year of Jesus' birth is a subject of debate among Christian scholars. In decades past it was believed that Jesus was born 3 or 2 B.C. and therefore was crucified and resurrected around age 33. Current New Testament scholarship places his birth at 4 B.C. (Ben Witherington III, *New Testament History*) or 6 or 5 B.C. (*Life Application Bible*). The order of the items listed on the timeline come from the "Summary of the Travels and Acts of Jesus" by Gordon Smith of Plenarth, United Kingdom. This material has not

yet been published, but it can be accessed on the Internet at the Christian Classics Ethereal Library at www.ccel.org/bible/phillips/JBPhillips.htm. The Web site is hosted by Calvin College, Grand Rapids, Michigan. The reader should be aware of the methodology Gordon used for his timeline. He wrote:

> The many different travels and acts of Jesus have been collected together and arranged to follow what are called "gospel harmonies." These attempt to place the events of Jesus' life in chronological order.
>
> Because the Gospels were written, not as historical biographies but as collections of teaching material aimed at different audiences—Jews, Romans, Greeks, the whole world—there will never be complete agreement between the harmonies.
>
> In arranging the Gospels in this way, any differences between various harmonies have been reconciled by making the following general assumptions:
>
> Mark's Gospel is in date order;
>
> Luke's Gospel is usually in date order, but there are discrepancies. These may be because he had to reconcile various eye-witness and written accounts;
>
> Matthew grouped some of his material to meet his teaching aims. His order is therefore not always chronological;
>
> The relationship of John's material to the three Synoptic Gospels has been developed by scholarly research over the last two centuries. Although there are still disagreements, these relationships are assumed to be generally reliable.

Gordon Smith, a retired engineer, is now a naval historian, author, and cruise lecturer who spent three years examining the Gospels in order to compile this information.

CHAPTER 10
THEIR MESSAGE TO THE WORLD

1. *The Correct Books of Bukhari*, vol. 4, bk. 56, no. 735.

2. Ibn Hisham, vol. 1, pt. 1, p. 302.

3. Ibn Hisham, vol. 3, pt. 6, p. 8.

4. *The Correct Books of Muslim*, bk. 1, no. 413.

5. *Sahih Muslim*, no. 2259.

6. *Sahih Muslim*, no. 1321. See also *The Correct Books of Muslim*, bk. 4, no. 1214.

7. *The Correct Books of Bukhari*, vol. 9, bk. 87, no. 145. Narrated by Kharija bin Zaid bin Thabit.

8. Dr. Haykyl, *Men Around the Messenger* (Cairo, Egypt: *Dar Al-Nahadah* Publishers, 1972).

9. *The Correct Books of Bukhari*, vol. 5, bk. 58, no. 245.

10. Haykyl, *Men Around the Messenger*.

11. *Sahih al-Bukhari*, no. 372, vol. 2, p. 208. See also *The Correct Books of Bukhari*, vol. 2, bk. 23, no. 372.

12. *The Correct Books of Bukhari*, vol. 4, bk. 55, no. 549. Narrated by Abdullah.

CHAPTER 11
THEIR TEACHINGS ABOUT EACH OTHER

1. *The Correct Books of Muslim*, bk. 30, no. 5836. See also *The Correct Books of Bukhari*, vol. 4, bk. 55, no. 652. Narrated by Abu Haraira.

2. See also *The Correct Books of Bukhari*, vol. 4, bk. 55, no. 644, where Muhammad describes Jesus as Allah's slave.

3. See also *The Correct Books of Bukhari*, vol. 6, bk. 60, no. 105.

5. *The Correct Books of Bukhari*, vol. 4, bk. 55, no. 654. Narrated by Umar.

6. These searches were done at the University of Southern California Web site. Their search engine incorporates three popular versions of the Quran.

7. *The Correct Books of Muslim*, bk. 26, no. 5428.

CHAPTER 12
HEALINGS AND MIRACLES

1. In the Quran, the word *We* is often used in reference to Allah. The word is used to convey a sense of greatness, not to imply that there is more than one god.

2. Ibn Kathir, *The Beginning and the End*, vol. 2, pt. 3, p. 190.

3. *The Correct Books of Muslim*, bk. 26, no. 5432.

4. Ibn Ishaq, p. 280. See also Ibn Hisham, vol. 2, pt. 3, pp. 132–133.

5. *The Correct Books of Bukhari*, vol. 2, bk. 23, no. 390. Narrated by Anas bin Malik.

6. Ibn Kathir in Arabic, *The Beginning and the End*, vol. 3, pt. 6, p. 154. Narrated by Ibn Abass.

7. *The Correct Books of Bukhari*, vol. 6, bk. 60, no. 390. Narrated by Anas.

8. Ibid., vol. 4, bk. 56, no. 780.

9. Ibid., vol. 4, bk. 56, no. 779.

10. Ibid., vol. 4, bk. 56, no. 777.

11. Ibid., vol. 1, bk. 7, no. 340.

12. Ibid., vol. 8, bk. 73, no. 115.

13. Ibid., vol. 1, bk. 8, no. 454.

14. Ibid., vol. 4, bk. 56, no. 783.

15. Ibid., vol. 4, bk. 56, no. 814.

16. Ibid., vol. 3, bk. 39, no. 517.

17. Ibid., vol. 5, bk. 58, no. 227.

CHAPTER 13
THE MEANING OF HOLY WAR

1. Al-Ghazali, *The Revival of Religious Science* (Beirut, Lebanon: *Dar al-Maharifa*), vol. 1, p. 172. Al-Ghazali lived in the twelfth century and was the founder of the Islamic Sufism movement. His book did not list the primary source for this anecdote.

2. Syed Maududi, The Meaning of the Quran, introduction to Surah 9, accessed at the University of Southern California Web site, http://www.usc.edu/dept/MSA/quran/maududi/mau9.html (accessed February 2, 2004).

3. Al-Nisai, vol. 3, pt. 6, p. 5, hadith no. 3,087. Narrated by Abu Hariara. Al-Nisai is one of the six correct books of hadith.

4. *The Correct Books of Muslim*, bk. 20, no. 4681. The tradition has been narrated on the authority of Abdullah b. Qais. He heard it from his father.

5. Ibn Hisham, vol. 2, pt. 4, p. 51.

6. Joey Green, *Jesus and Muhammad: The Parallel Sayings* (Berkeley, CA: Ulysses Press, 2003).

CHAPTER 14
TEACHINGS ABOUT LOVE

1. *The Correct Books of Bukhari*, vol. 8, bk. 81, no. 768. Narrated by Abu Salama.

2. Ibid., vol. 8, bk. 81, no. 778. Narrated by Aisha.

CHAPTER 15
TEACHINGS ON PRAYER

1. *The Correct Books of Bukhari*, vol. 1, bk. 8, no. 345.

2. Times are also calculated according to different systems, so they can vary from one mosque to another.

3. *The Correct Books of Bukhari*, vol. 1, bk. 11, no. 617. Narrated by Abu Haraira.

4. Ibid., vol. 4, bk. 54, no. 492. Narrated by Abdullah.

5. Sunan ibn Majah, vol. 1, p. 412. This is one of the six correct books of hadith.

6. You can offer nephil prayer before or after the first time of prayer, but not again until the call for the second prayer. You can do extra raka'ah between the second and third prayer, but not between the third and fourth prayer. Finally, extra raka'ahs are allowed between fourth and fifth prayer and all night between fifth prayer and first prayer.

7. *The Correct Books of Muslim*, bk. 4, no. 1366.

CHAPTER 16
ATTITUDES TOWARD WOMEN

1. *The Correct Books of Bukhari*, vol. 8, bk. 76, no. 456. Narrated by 'Imran bin Husain.

2. *The Correct Books of Muslim*, bk. 4, no. 1032. Narrated by Abu Dharr.

3. *The Correct Books of Bukhari*, vol. 1, bk. 9, no. 490. Narrated by Aisha.

4. Ibid., vol. 7, bk. 62, no. 31. Narrated by Ibn Umar.

5. Ibid., vol. 1, bk. 6, no. 301. Narrated by Abu Said Al-Khudri.

6. Ibid., vol. 3, bk. 48, no. 826. Narrated by Abu Said Al-Khudri.

7. Ibid., vol. 6, bk. 60, no. 317.

8. Ibid., vol. 6, bk. 60, no. 313.

9. Ibid., vol. 6, bk. 60, no. 282. Narrated by Safiya bint Shaiba.

10. *The Correct Books of Muslim*, bk. 8, no. 3432. Narrated by Abu Sa'id al-Khudri. See also *Sahih Muslim*, vol. 2, pt. 2, no. 3608.

11. *The Correct Books of Bukhari*, vol. 7, bk. 62, no. 121. Narrated by Abu Huraira. See also *Sahih al-Bukhari*, no. 3608.

12. For example, see *The Correct Books of Muslim*, bk. 9, no. 3527.

13. *The Correct Books of Bukhari*, vol. 7, bk. 62, no. 88. Narrated by Ursa.

14. Ibid., vol. 6, bk. 60, no. 274. Narrated by Aisha.

15. Ibn Kathir, *The Quran Commentary* (Mansura, Egypt: Faith Library, 1996), vol. 3, pt. 6, p. 239.

16. *The Correct Books of Bukhari*, vol. 9, bk. 93, no. 516. Narrated by Anas.

17. Ibn Jarir, *The History of Messengers and Kings*, vol 3, p. 251. See also *The Correct Books of Bukhari*, vol. 2, bk. 14, no. 8.

18. *The Correct Books of Bukhari*, vol. 4, bk. 52, no. 143 and Ibn Ishaq in English, p. 511.

19. Ibn Ishaq, p. 517.

20. Ibn Kathir, *The Beginning and the End*.

21. Ibid.

22. Ibid.

23. *The Correct Books of Muslim*, bk. 9, no. 3498 and 3506. See also *The Correct Books of Bukhari*, vol. 6, bk. 60, no. 309.

CHAPTER 17
INTERESTING COINCIDENCES

1. *The Correct Books of Muslim*, bk. 17, no. 4206, author's paraphrase.

2. Abu Mawdudi, *Introduction to the Surahs*, Surah 80.

3. Ibn Ishaq, pp. 569–570. See also Surah 9:25–26.

4. Ibn Hisham, vol. 1, pt. 2, p. 222.

CHAPTER 18
A COMPARISON OF PRACTICAL TEACHINGS

1. *The Correct Books of Muslim*, bk. 17, no. 4230; also see *Sahih Muslim*, vol. 3.

2. Ibid., bk. 1, no. 79. Narrated on the authority of Tariq b. Shihab.

3. *The Correct Books of Bukhari*, vol. 9, bk. 92, no. 445. Narrated by Ibn 'Umar. See also *Sahih al-Bukhari*, vol. 4, no. 6614.

APPENDIX A
THE SOURCES OF INFORMATION ABOUT
JESUS AND MUHAMMAD

1. See *Correct Books of Bukhari*, vol. 8, bk. 81, no. 768 for this story.

2. Introductions to the translations of *The Correct Books of Bukhari* and *The Correct Books of Muslim* on the University of Southern California Web site (accessed December 17, 2003).

3. Al-Tabari, *The History of the Kings and the Prophets*.

4. Lee Strobel, *The Case for Christ* (Zondervan: Grand Rapids, MI, 1998), p. 59. The information provided is based on his interview with renowned New Testament scholar Bruce Metzger.

5. *Life Application Bible* (Wheaton, IL: Tyndale House, 1998). See the introduction to each Gospel.

APPENDIX B
ISLAMIC TEACHING REGARDING
BIBLICAL PROPHECIES ABOUT MUHAMMAD

1. *The Noble Quran*, footnote to Surah 7:157.

Bibliography

English Language

Ibn Ishaq. *The Life of Muhammad: A Translation of Ibn Ishaq's Sirat Rasul Allah.* Translated by A. Guillaume. Karachi, Pakistan: Oxford University Press, 16th printing, 2003. This is the English translation of the book referred to in the Arabic section of this bibliography as Ibn Hisham. Ibn Hisham was a man who came a few years after Ibn Ishaq and added some notes to his book. Muslims refer to this work by saying either Ibn Ishaq or Ibn Hisham.

Jeffrey, Grant R. *Jesus: The Great Debate.* Nashville, TN: Word, 1999.

Life Application Bible. Arabic version. Netherlands: Tyndale House Publishers, 1999.

Sahih al-Bukhari (The Correct Books of Bukhari). English translation by Dr. Muhammad Muhasin Khan. Material was accessed at the University of Southern California Web site, 2003.

Sahih Muslim (The Correct Books of Muslim). English translation by Abdul Hamid Siddiqui. Two recent publishers: Kitab Bhaven, New Delhi, India, 2000 and Kazi Publications in Chicago, IL, 1976. Material was accessed at the University of Southern California Web site, 2003.

Strobel, Lee. *The Case for Christ.* Grand Rapids, MI: Zondervan, 1998.

The Holy Bible, New International Version. Grand Rapids, MI: Zondervan, 1973, 1978, 1984.

Arabic Language

Ibn Hisham. *The Life of Muhammad*, 3rd ed. Beruit, Lebanon: *Dar-al-Jil*, 1998. This is the same book as the one referenced by the name Ibn Ishaq under the English language section of this bibliography.

Ibn Kathir. *The Beginning and the End.* Beruit, Lebanon: The Revival of the Arabic Tradition Publishing House, 2001.

Bibliography

Sahih al-Bukhari. Translated by Muhammad Muhsin Khan. Mecca, Saudi Arabia: The House of Revival of the Tradition of the Prophethood, A.H. 1398 (1978). This book contains both Arabic and English.

Sahih Muslim. Riyadh, Saudi Arabia: Peace Publishing House, 1999.

Shalaby, Dr. A. *Encyclopedia of Islamic History.* Cairo, Egypt: *dar al-Nahadah*, 1973.

Index

Author's Academic Credentials

Dr. Gabriel's academic credentials in Islamic scholarship include:

- Bachelor's, master's, and doctorate degrees in Islamic History and Culture from Al-Azhar University, Cairo, Egypt

- Graduating second in his class of six thousand students for his bachelor's degree. This ranking was based on cumulative scores of oral and written exams given at the end of each school year.

- One of the youngest lecturers ever hired at Al-Azhar University. He started lecturing after he finished his master's degree and was working to finish his doctorate.

- Traveling lecturer. The university sent him to countries around the Middle East as a lecturer in Islamic history.

Al-Azhar University is the most respected, authoritative Islamic university in the world. It has been in continuous operation for more than one thousand years.

In addition to his academic training, Dr. Gabriel had practical experience, serving as the imam at a mosque in the Cairo suburbs.

After Dr. Gabriel became a Christian, he pursued a Christian education. His credentials in Christian education include:

- Discipleship Training School with Youth With A Mission in Cape Town, South Africa.

- Master's degree in World Religion from Florida Christian University in Orlando, Florida (2001).

- Doctorate degree in Christian Education from Florida Christian University in Orlando, Florida (2002).

- Induction as a fellow in the Oxford Society of Scholars, September 2003.